TRUSTED

THE
LEVEL
ABOVE
INFLUENCE

JANE ANDERSON

Cover Design and copy editing: Lauren Shay, Full Stop Publishing
Internal design: Olivier Darbonville

Acknowledgements |

I've never had children but every book I write seems to be like giving birth. From the original idea to final production takes about nine months, but this one took longer. I had been planning on writing my next book (not this one) and the concepts in this book kept pushing me back. I felt like I was in a boxing ring and every time I tried to write, it would come up with a left hook and smash me on the mat. It sounds harsh but it was like I couldn't work on anything else until this piece of work was completed.

After meeting with a series of mentors, including Matt Church, Dan Gregory and Kieran Flanagan, and grappling with it, I'm so pleased it is now finally in a format people can use!

To the masters of their craft and my second family – Rowdy McLean, Keith Abraham and Amanda Stevens, who have had such an impact on me and every idea in this book. They pushed me far beyond what I could have achieved on my own. This would not have happened without you.

To the clients I see every day. We work on every aspect of this book in their practices and they are such an inspiration with the ripple they create in the world. I am grateful to see their work behind the scenes and their unwavering commitment to helping their tribes achieve their potential.

To the team closest to me, which makes projects like this come to life. My partner, Mark, who is one of the smartest and kindest human beings on the planet. His support, along with the support of my family, has been unconditional. The late-night proofreading, listening to and challenging my ideas have been beyond invaluable. Thank you to you all for your patience and making this come to life.

Finally, to my support team in the office—Virginia, Rhia and Trinsa, who share my vision to create change, educate, innovate and help people grow to become the best leaders they can be.

Finally, to the editing and publishing team —Lauren Shay at Full Stop Writing, Editing and Design, my 'to be' Father-In Law Carl Smith, and Sylvie Blair at BookPOD. Thank you for your commitment and dedication and being part of the team for every book project to date. Without you, these ideas don't see the light of day.

Table of Contents |

Introduction |

I recently went to a dry cleaners and alterations shop as I desperately wanted the neckline of a dress changed. A friend of mine had the same dress and had managed to get her hemline fixed. The dress cost a lot of money, so I wanted to ensure it didn't get damaged.

The lady in the alterations shop asked me to put the dress on and show her what I wanted to be done. As I did, she ummed and ahhed. She said I'd have to lose some fabric in the neckline, which I didn't want to happen. Besides, my friend didn't have to lose any on hers. I questioned the lady about it, and she asked me to wait so she could get her boss for advice.

He came out in a beautifully cut shirt and pants. His clothes fitted him perfectly, like they were made for him. I showed him what I wanted and explained it was an expensive dress. He took some measurements and said it would be fine; he could alter it without losing any fabric. I was thrilled. Judging by how well his clothes fitted, I knew I was in safe hands. And I was.

This was just one interaction in one day. There are so many times when we interact with a sense of trust. The computer you bought, this book you're reading, your health insurance provider, your car. You use all these things because you trust they can do the job and will deliver on the promise made when you bought them.

I have spent my career working for highly trusted brands and people—from personally branded businesses to award-winning CEOs and some of the world's leading experts in their fields. I help them maintain trust, rebuild it when it's lost or build their brand from scratch. I leverage trust for their growth. Some don't realise how much trust they already have and fail to see their opportunities. Others think they have more trust in their brand than they actually do and need some tough love. Either way, when we work with customers, clients, team members and our community, particularly during times of change, trust is the currency.

So, why have I chosen to write about this topic of trust?

Generally, I've found people are very open with me. They are quick to trust me and share deeply personal information—their fears, challenges, hopes and dreams. For a long time, I thought everyone was able to connect at this level, but it wasn't until people asked me how I did it that I realised I could grow my business more than I had thought. I suddenly realised I had built enough trust as a leader, influencer and branding expert. So, after being asked to teach on the subject, I decided to assist other leaders trying to create more influence in their businesses and careers.

When you have trust, you have leverage—leverage to create whatever you want. I believe leverage creates true personal power and freedom— freedom to be yourself, freedom to be with the people you want to be with, freedom to be creative and the freedom to become the best version of you.

There are times when I have had to go through a lot of personal growth and change, and I have had to lean on those I trust to give me the right advice and pave the way ahead.

Being a trusted leader is one of the most powerful gifts you can give to family, friends, your community and your team.

A huge thank you to the people I trust, whose love, guidance and support have made it possible for me to create this book: Matt Church, Keith Abraham, Rowdy McLean, Amanda Stevens, Peter Cook, Dan Gregory, Kieran Flanagan and all my amazing clients, my family and Mark.

Why Trust Matters

CHAPTER ONE

"The best way you can find out
whether you can trust somebody
is to trust them."

– Ernest Hemingway

I remember it like it was yesterday.

I came home from being away with friends for the weekend, and I could immediately tell something was wrong.

My then-husband was verbally attacking me for no reason. He was angry and I started to realise something was seriously wrong. My instincts told me he'd been unfaithful; I don't know what, but I just felt an inkling. I'd never seen or experienced behaviour from him like this, so I asked him. And he owned up.

While the sudden purging of the truth was a release for him and made him feel free, I was not. I was left grappling with the reality of what was happening.

I was in disbelief. Yet I also experienced a strange feeling of understanding, that I had seen it coming for some time but couldn't stop it.

I moved in with a girlfriend to get some space and try to work out what to do. Do I leave town and start a new life? Or do I stick it out? Everything kept coming back to trust.

Could I ever trust this person again?

I decided to stay in town and leave no stone unturned to find the answer to that question. I read every book in the library, I spoke to counsellors, mentors, my boss, even a priest. What I didn't do was contact my family. They despised my husband and saw his behaviour a long way off before I did. I was so ashamed and embarrassed by not only his behaviour but also by my decision to marry this person.

So, at the three-month mark to the day, I decided to go. I knew I couldn't trust this person any longer.

About a year later, I started to date again and realised I was not ready. I wasn't meeting the right people, and it was frustrating. I got to a point where I couldn't trust myself any more. My own decisions were failing me. I also decided I never wanted to go through a divorce again, so I chose to work with a coach to help me understand more about myself.

My coach made me realise that everything I had been teaching others about trust in their leadership and branding could be applied to personal relationships. So, for the next three years, I undertook a lot of deep work around what builds trust at the most human level. I decided to take what I knew from years of marketing, leadership and communication for brands and businesses, and identify the elements that create rock-solid relationships between brands and customers, and apply them to a relationship with another human being.

As a result of this deeply personal and business-related work, I have not only found an incredible partner in my life and become engaged, but also started to work with some of the world's most respected experts in their field, helping them to build their personal brands.

I realised the currency that was most important to me and every consumer on the planet was trust.

As leaders, we're all in the business of relationships, and relationships are all about trust. Whether you're leading a team or dealing with stakeholders, trust is paramount.

So, why does it matter in business today?

Trust has changed

In late January 1998, the then US president Bill Clinton gave his infamous speech about his dealings with a White House intern, 22-year-old Monica Lewinsky. The scandal had rocked Clinton's reputation, and he stated, "I did not have sexual relations with that woman." We now know he was lying, and with it came a watershed moment that a prestigious authority —a president— would lie.

Around the same time, the internet became available to the public. With access to so much information (and misinformation), the way people consumed information and made decisions quickly evolved—and continues to evolve. Today, we can "Google" symptoms when we feel unwell, search for people's background information and find out more about any subject than ever before. This has created increased transparency. Instead of the media filtering conversations, social media has given the average person a voice.

As a result, we have become aware of others' opinions and question "whom do I trust?".

When trying to identify whom they can trust, customers no longer look for certificates on walls. They look for social proof, such as an online presence and customer reviews on Google and Facebook. They're trying to find out who has the real influence, the real power and who is the real deal.

OLD TRUST	NEW TRUST
Certificates	Results
Networks	Reputation
Testimonials	Reviews
Transactions	Tribes
Products	Humans
Popular	Connected
Marketing	Education
Perfect	Authentic

As a result, leaders and businesses have moved away from formal ways of building trust to far more socially connected and socially proven methods of building trust.

The world is changing

The world is going through incredible change and disruption. In the past year, we have seen some extraordinary global shifts, including:

• Saudi Arabia granted women the right to apply for a driver's licence.

• Hawaii's Kilauea volcano erupted, delivering a dazzling display of nature's might and redesigning the map of Hawaii's Big Island.

• The US, under the reign of President Donald Trump, announced it would withdraw from the United Nations Human Rights Council.

• Canada became the first major industrialised country to legalise cannabis for recreational use.

• Apple Inc. became the world's first public company to achieve a market capitalisation of $1 trillion.

• 700,000 people marched through central London, demanding a second referendum on the final Brexit deal. The event was the second-most attended protest of the 21st century in the United Kingdom, after the "Stop the War" anti-Iraq War march in 2003.

• The CEO of Tesla, Elon Musk, launched his car into space.

• More than 5 million women across India formed a human chain for 620km to create a mass demonstration for gender equality.

• Facebook, the world's largest social media networking platform, was involved in a major political scandal with Cambridge Analytica after it was found to have harvested data for political purposes without the permission of profile owners.

• The #metoo movement and the spotlight on the Catholic Church and other institutions highlighted the widespread abuse of power.

When we have so much disruption and change, we need to create societies and workplaces that can adapt. The only way to adapt quickly is to have high trust. Without trust, the speed of change slows, causing angst, fear, stress and chaos.

Why trust matters in the world

Trust is essential to a cohesive society. It holds cultures together, and it maintains order.

Different countries have different levels of trust. Each year, the Foreign Corruption Practices Act identifies 14 indicators of societal trustworthiness, including corruption, competition, reputation, sustainability, economic freedom, healthcare and women's rights.[1] Combining the findings and totalling the scores, Trust Across America created the 2018 Country Trust Index™.[2] Almost 70 countries were analysed, with scores ranging from 66 to 1432. The lower the score, the higher the country ranked.

Switzerland won by a landslide, scoring a Trust Index of 66 and ranking in the top five countries in 10 of the 14 categories. Its lowest score was in healthcare, ranking #20.

After Switzerland, the scores dropped steeply. The top 10 countries and their scores were:

- Switzerland – **66**
- Norway – **102**
- Denmark – **119**
- Canada – **120**
- Sweden – **125**
- Finland – **131**
- New Zealand – **137**
- Netherlands – **139**
- Australia – **170**
- Austria – **195**

The United States trailed the top 10 at #20, with a total score of 369 and a poor showing on reputation, healthcare and safety.

The following countries represented the bottom Trust Index rankings:

- Saudi Arabia – **929**
- Brazil – **958**
- India – **978**
- China – **1004**
- Vietnam – **1048**
- Russia – **1062**
- Ukraine – **1245**
- Egypt – **1274**
- Pakistan – **1370**
- Nigeria – **1432**

The purpose of the Trust Index was to highlight the "best in breed". Whether we're talking about countries, businesses or leaders, "elevating trust and ethics is a win/win for all stakeholders".[3]

How trust is measured

Researchers McEliry and Wood, in the Journal of Trust Research, undertook a major review of all trust measurements and assessments in organisations. Currently, more than 100 different measures of trust are used globally to assess various aspects of trust for leaders, individuals and organisations.[4]

Five noteworthy measures include:

AUTHORS	MEASUREMENT INSTRUMENT
McAllister (1995)	*Managerial Interpersonal Trust*
Currall and Judge (1995)	*Boundary Role Person's Trust*
Cummings and Bromiley (1996)	*Organisational Trust Inventory*
Mayer and Davis (1999)	*Organisational Trust*
Gillespie (2003)	*Behavioural Trust Inventory*

The fact that there are so many measures created by so many researchers indicates the need for a greater understanding of trust and how it impacts individuals, businesses and cultures. Each measure has its merits, and deciding on which one to use depends on its relevance to the application. Regardless, the value in measuring trust means taking active steps to increase it.

Why trust matters for industries

Year on year, the industries and professions that have the most trust are the emergency services, the military, nurses, doctors and paramedics. The least-trusted professionals are real estate agents and car salesmen.[5]

According to Roy Morgan research into Australia's most trusted industry-specific brands[6]:

• Bendigo Bank is ranked as Australia's most trusted bank.

	0	10	20	30	40	50	60	70	80	90	100
Nurses											94
Doctors										89	
Pharmacists									84		
School Teachers									81		
Engineers									80		
Dentists									79		
Police								76			
High Court Judges								74			
State Supreme Court Judges								71			
University Lecturers							66				
Accountants						50					
Public Servants				37							
Lawyers				35							
Public Opinion Pollsters				34							
Ministers of Religion				34							
Bank Managers				33							
Directors of Public Companies			25								
Financial Planners			25								
Newspaper Journalists			20								
Business Executives			18								
Union Leaders		17									
TV Reporters		17									
Federal MPs		16									
State MPs		16									
Talk-back Radio Announcers		14									
Stockbrokers		11									
Insurance Brokers		10									
Real Estate Agents	7										
Advertising People	5										
Car Salesmen	4										

% of Australians aged 14+ rating the profession as 'very high' or 'high' for ethics and honesty

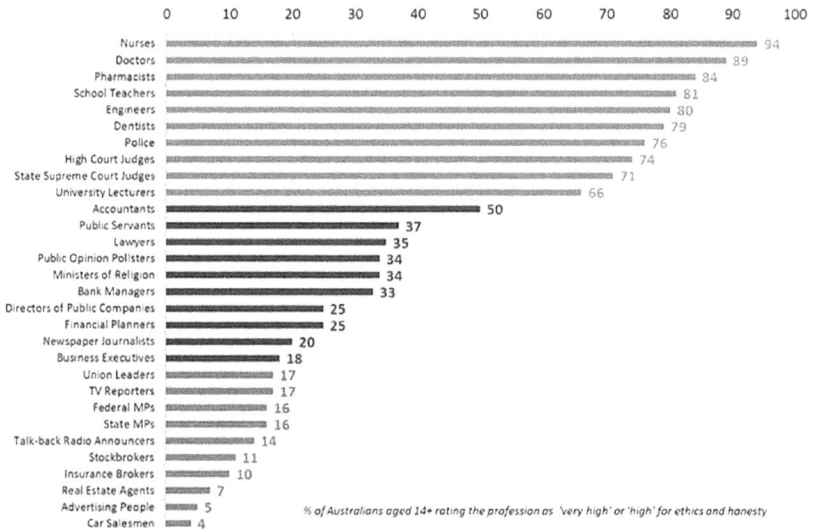

Source: Roy Morgan Image of Professions surveys of Australians 14+ between 1976 – 2017.

• HCF is ranked as the most trusted private health insurer.

• Netball is the most trusted sport.

• The ABC is the most trusted media brand.

• SBS is the most trusted commercial media brand.

And Australia's most trusted brands are:

1. Aldi

2. Bunnings

3. Qantas

The impact of a lack of trust for industries is disruption. Let's look at some of these industries.

Insurance and finance

According to the Insurance Council of Australia, cyber insurance is the fastest-growing commercial segment in the Australian market, with coverage increasingly incorporated into business insurance packages or sold as an individual product.[7] What will be the impact of services such as robo advice (digital financial product advice or automated advice) when trust is already low? People tend to change providers or look for better options when they feel less committed to providers.

Australia is experiencing the aftermath of findings form the Royal Commission into the banking secitor It comes as no surprise that fewer than one in three Australians have a high level of trust in banks.[8] Australian Bankers Association chief Anna Bligh argues that the sector's new code of conduct will help plug the trust gap, but can a code of conduct truly help an industry achieve its potential when it comes to rebuilding trust?

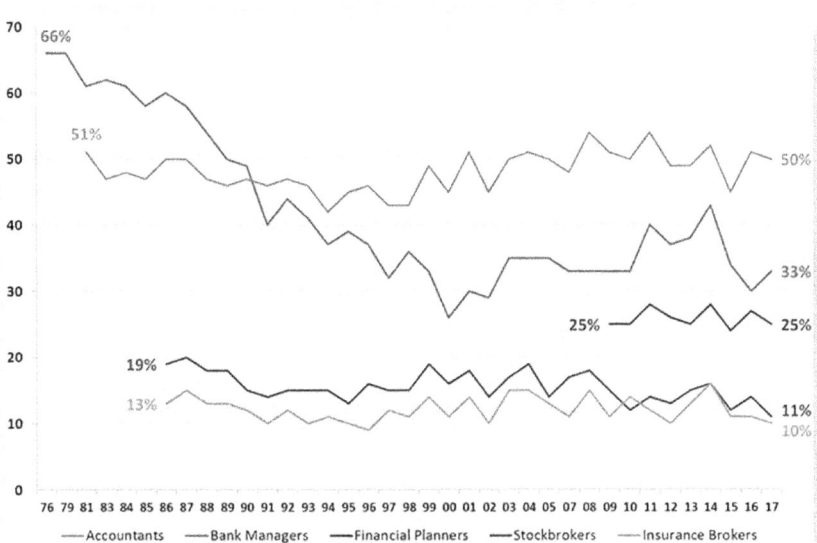

Source: Roy Morgan Image of Professions surveys of Australians 14+ between 1976 – 2017

Over two days of questioning at the Royal Commission in 2018, AMP Advice Executive Jack Regan confessed to no fewer than 20 separate occasions when AMP misled the corporate regulator over charging its financial advice clients "fees for no service".[9] The Commonwealth Bank also confessed to charging fees to dead people.[10] And Westpac admitted it had paid bonuses to a financial adviser it knew was churning clients into high-fee investments.

By the week's end, heads began to roll. AMP's CEO Craig Meller resigned, effective immediately after his interrogation.[11] Back-flipping on his previous resistance to a royal commission,[12] Federal Treasurer Scott Morrison announced increased penalties of up to 10 years' jail for white-collar crimes.[13] And this time, it was the banks that were on notice.

Banks and financial institutions have a long road ahead of them when it comes to rebuilding trust. Bendigo Bank is the only bank to have maintained its positive score[14] amongst the banks in the Royal Commission.

Health

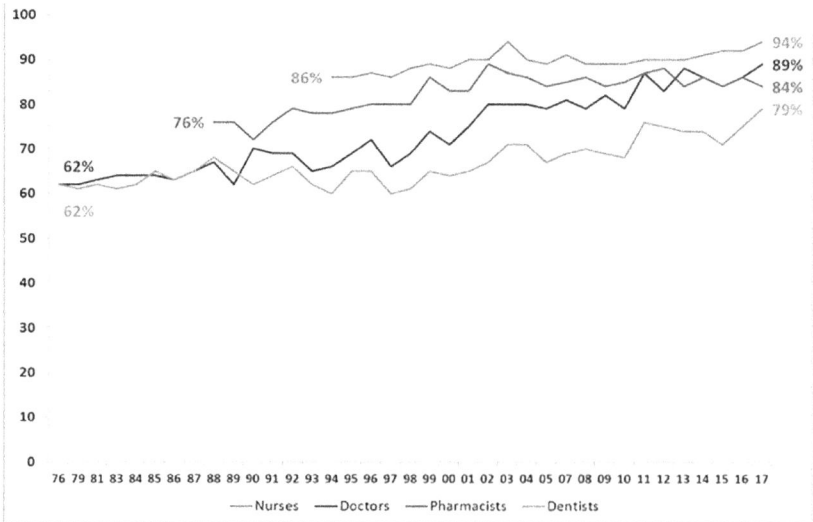

Source: Roy Morgan Image of Professions surveys of Australians 14+ between 1976 – 2017

Social media and the public's access to a wealth of health information (and misinformation) online means people are turning to trusted healthcare experts more often. Advances in technology, funding, education, and research and the fact that people are living for longer all work to position the industry in an upward trend for building trust.

Religion

One of the industries most affected by a lack of trust is religion. Trust in this industry continues to fall after the Royal Commission into Institutional Responses to Child Sexual Abuse. It seems there is a media report almost daily about the abuse of power and trust in the Catholic Church. The church was once a place where people united as a community and connected with their values. But with the negative publicity, people are becoming more fearful of being involved with these institutions.

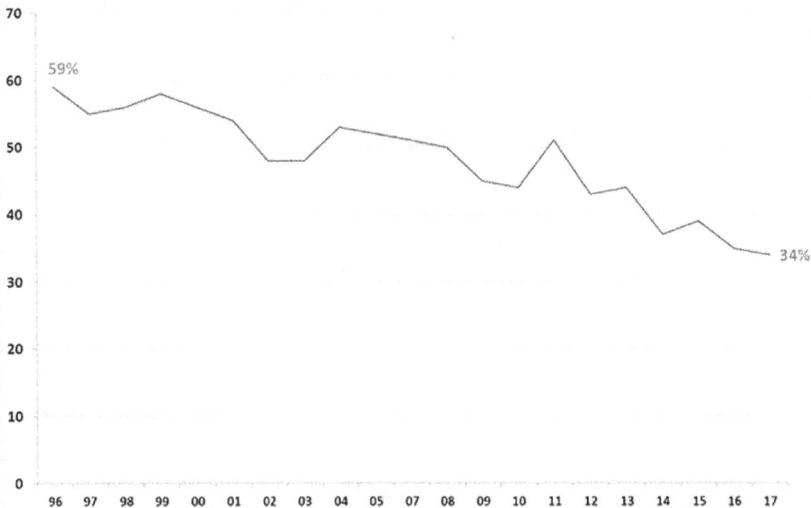

Source: Roy Morgan Image of Professions surveys of Australians 14+ between 1976 – 2017

Why trust matters for organisations

In 2016, the Thunder River Rapids ride at the amusement park Dreamworld, in Queensland, experienced a mechanical failure that resulted in the deaths of four people. Forty-eight hours later, the board for Ardent Leisure (the owners of Dreamworld) held its Annual General Meeting as if nothing had happened. The CFO was forced to defend the bonus payment of $843,000 to CEO Deborah Thomas,[15] promising to hold a memorial for the victims and "donate funds to the Red Cross".

Thomas said Ardent had made contact with the family of Kim Dorsett, whose two children, Kate Goodchild and Luke Dorsett, were among the four victims. But it turned out Thomas hadn't spoken to them, much to the fury and dismay of the family. A journalist had to provide Thomas Dorsett's mobile phone number. There was a public outcry demanding Thomas not accept her bonus payment or at least give it to the victims of the incident.

This was not just a communications shamble. It was a moral and ethical disgrace. All trust in the leadership of the amusement park, which had been a favourite of families for decades, had been lost. Ardent Leisure is now on the journey to rebuild the brand of Dreamworld and the reputation of the board. This is a prime example of a brand that shifted rapidly from influence to disengagement as a result of lost trust and human connection.

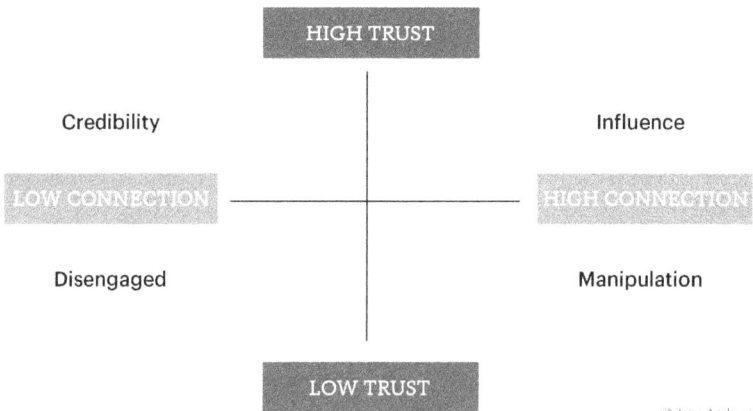

© Jane Anderson

According to a 2002 study by Watson Wyatt, organisations considered to be high-trust outperformed low-trust organisations by 286 per cent in total return to shareholders.[16] Furthermore, a study by Russell Investment Group in 2005 showed that **Fortune** magazine's "100 Best Companies to Work for", in which trust comprised 60 per cent of the criteria, earned more than four times the returns of the broader market over the seven years prior.[17]

In addition, a PricewaterhouseCoopers (PwC) study of corporate innovation among the Financial Times 100 index showed that "the number-one differentiating factor between the top innovators and the bottom innovators was trust."[18] So, as you can see, having trust creates a formidable platform to drive change.

It's also interesting to note that a 10 per cent increase in trust between a manager and an employee has the equivalent effect on life satisfaction as a 36 per cent increase in income.[19]

This highlights two points that I regularly teach my clients:

1. Don't be deluded into thinking your employees are motivated by money; they are not. They may go looking for more money but what causes their initial dissatisfaction with their job rarely has anything to do with money.

2. Smart companies put their training and employee engagement dollars towards increasing the capability of their managers and teaching them the skills to build trust between themselves and their teams.

In his book, **First Things First,**[20] Stephen Covey says three significant factors slow the business growth of low-trust organisations:

1. Span of control

• Hovering and double checking take time and energy.

• High-trust culture doesn't need to hover and double check.

• Low trust culture is 1 supervisor to every 10 people, high trust is 1 supervisor to 50 people.

2. Motivation

• Low-trust culture puts a carrot out front to motivate people.

• In a high-trust culture, people are internally motivated and have passion, a shared vision and synergy.

3. Structure and systems

• Low-trust culture is full of bureaucracy, duplication, rules and regulations, and restrictive closed systems.

• Low initiative, a "do as you're told" mentality and a quarterly bottom line drive the culture.

• High-trust structures and systems empower, liberate, create energy and foster creativity. There's less bureaucracy, fewer rules and more involvement.

Engagement scores

According to organisational psychologist and researcher Jessica Pryce-Jones, organisations with fewer than 1000 employees traditionally have higher engagement scores. In her book, *Happiness at Work: Maximizing Your Psychological Capital for Success,* Pryce-Jones says organisations that focus on the happiness and well-being of their staff are more likely to have high engagement scores.[21]

Doing more with less

Trust is all about speed. Today, organisations need to be agile enough to navigate disruption and change. As a consequence of the 2007-2009 global financial crisis, many organisations became much leaner. In Queensland alone, more than 14,000 public servants were made redundant.

In 2012, Australia saw a significant shift towards organisations recruiting fewer staff and more contractors, project-based workers and specialists. They were trying to find better and faster ways of doing work while navigating the overwhelm of information and noise.

When organisations are pulled in various directions due to small- and large-scale change, people and teams can start to become resentful. However, when an organisation has a culture of high trust, teams and individuals are more likely to survive such dramatic shifts.

Maintaining a solid platform of trust during change has many benefits, including:

1. Problems are solved faster.

2. Teams are built more efficiently.

3. Relationships grow authentically

4. Higher levels of performance emerge.

The importance of trust for CEOs

In 2002, Jack Ma Yun, co-founder of the Alibaba Group, recruited Tong Wenhong as a receptionist.[22] When Ma was allocating company shares, he asked Tong to remain with the company and gave her 0.2 per cent in shares, assuring her it would be worth $100 billion when Alibaba went public on the New York Stock Exchange.

Tong waited, but Alibaba didn't go public. In 2004, she asked Ma when it would happen, and he told her "soon". She asked again in 2006, and Ma again said "soon". When Alibaba finally went public in September 2014, it was worth $245.7 billion. Tong, by then a former senior receptionist and current vice president of Alibaba, became a millionaire with $320 million.

Ma knew how difficult it was to find and retain great talent. He needed someone competent, like Tong, to support him in the long haul. In fact, according to Kenneth Freeman from the Boston University of Management, the top five challenges for CEOs globally are:[23]

1. Finding and retaining talent

2. Disruptive technology

3. Globalisation

4. Cybersecurity

5. Uncertainty

In 2018, PwC published its Future of Work 2030 report.[24] It identified disruption as being a constant challenge for organisations for the next 10 to 15 years. This means leaders and CEOs need to focus less on disruption and more on building strong trust in their organisations. Trust is the key to increasing the speed and agility leaders and teams need to navigate the constant changes they face.

CEOs are starting to take greater notice of reputation and brand. The 2017 KPMG Global CEO survey found that brand and reputation risk were among the top three concerns and impacts for CEOs regarding business growth.[25] Brand and reputation had not previously ranked in the top 10 concerns in the annual report.

So, there is no doubt that trust is more relevant now than ever as the environment and dynamics of today's world and workplace continue to change dramatically.

Why trust matters for leaders

Leaders need to find ways to increase connection and influence to motivate their teams and improve speed and performance. As organisational leadership expert John Maxwell says: "The beauty of trust is that it erases worry and frees you to get on with other matters. Trust means confidence."

Some of the emerging trends and challenges affecting trust for leaders include:

• **Managing remote teams:** more demand for flexible work arrangements including working from home and recruitment of offshore talent.

• **High-performance teams:** We're in the age of the super worker, trying to find ways to increase performance and embracing new practices such as biohacking.

• **Time:** doing more with less, keeping with the speed of change and dealing with overwhelm.

• **Lean Organisations:** Since the Global Financial Crisis in 2008 organisations are carrying less excess staff and employing more project-based teams.

For leaders to be effective in their role, trust is paramount. But how many employees trust their managers?

A recent study by Edelman found that one in three employees didn't trust their manager. However, another study by EY found that number to be even lower, with only 46 per cent having trust in their organisation and 49 per cent in their boss/team.[26]

Trust is critical in the workplace. Without it, you won't have the environment you need for an effective feedback culture to grow.

In her book, Presence, Harvard Business School professor and TED speaker Amy Cuddy says the two questions people ask themselves when they first meet someone are:[27]

• *Do I trust you*

• *Do I respect you?*

Psychologists say these questions link to the dimensions of warmth and competence. Ideally, as a leader, you will be perceived as having a mix of both. Cuddy says that people often think it's competence that builds trust; but, it's the blend of these two qualities that creates real influence. Cuddy's research found that competence is only assessed once a person has decided whether they trust you. For many leaders, it's easy to fixate on appearing competent in the role, but Cuddy says:

> *If someone you're trying to influence doesn't trust you, you're not going to get very far; in fact, you might even elicit suspicion because you come across as manipulative. A warm, trustworthy person who is also strong elicits admiration, but only after you've established trust, does your strength become a gift rather than a threat.*

However, some leaders assume power due to their title. A great example is Donald Trump. As President of the US, he has immense power, but overall, the sentiment is that he isn't trustworthy.

When a leader erodes trust, the impacts are far-reaching and can lead to wasted time, resources, effort and energy, not to mention talent loss. According to the Harvard Business Review, the two critical factors that erode trust for leaders are: [28]

• **Lack of self-awareness.** This means a lack of control. People want to know you can handle yourself and overcome the challenges you face.

• **Bottom-line mentality.** Focusing only on revenue and profit shows little understanding, empathy and insight into what people experience in their roles, especially when going through dynamic change.

Why trust matters for your customers

In 2018, Accenture published a research report into the financial impacts of a lack of trust in organisations. It found that 54 per cent of the companies examined had experienced a material drop in trust in the past two-and-a-half years. The average company that experienced that drop saw their Competitive Agility Index score decline by two points, with the revenues at stake equating to at least US$180 billion.[29]

Michael Lyman, Senior Managing Director at Accenture Strategy, North American Lead, said:

> *Our research proves that no company is immune to the impact of a drop in trust on the bottom line. US companies must adopt a top-down culture that fully bakes trust into the company's strategy, operations and broader DNA. Those who don't are putting their future revenues at risk.*

Trust is no longer a soft skill for business growth. Today, it is highly tangible.

Given that "trust incidents" (e.g. consumer data theft, tainted food, cyber breaches) are on the rise, Accenture says companies need to develop an interdependent strategy that combines growth, profitability and trust if they are to compete on an ongoing basis.

Rohit Bhargava, the author of the popular Non-Obvious Trends report, recently published a preview of his 2019 Non-Obvious Trends. In the preview, he highlights an emerging trend he calls "RetroTrust".[30] As customers become increasingly sceptical of the motives of brands, they are defaulting to brands that have a legacy, those they have a personal history with and, by implication, those they trust.

Again, trust is far more important to consumers now that they have an unprecedented amount of choice and access to information.

We're living in a digital-first world

In his book ***Ctrl Alt Delete,*** Mitch Joel discusses the term "digital first". He reveals the five fundamental movements organisations must embrace to future-proof themselves – or go out of business. One of these shifts is the fact that now, the first place your brand and business are validated is online. The internet has the power to make or break your chances of success.

Serial entrepreneur Gary Vaynerchuk is an excellent example of how to cultivate a successful business by leveraging digital media. Born in the Soviet Union in 1975, Vaynerchuk immigrated to the United States in 1978. From humble beginnings, his father went on to own a liquor store in New Jersey. In the early days of the digital-first world, Vaynerchuk could see the burning potential of his father's business. After graduating from college, Vaynerchuk transformed the liquor shop into a retail wine store, which he named the "Wine Library". In 2006, he started a daily video blog, **Wine Library TV.** This hugely popular webcast turned him into an internet celebrity. It attracted 90,000 viewers a day and led to a flurry of TV and speaking engagements. In just six years, Vaynerchuk grew the family business from $1 million a year to a whopping $50 million a year!

Not too bad for a small family business, right?

So, as you can see, traditional marketing has been blown out of the water. We're no longer restricted to cold calling and setting up meeting after meeting to generate leads and sales. Digital marketing has opened an array of cost-effective avenues for self-promotion and lead generation. Sales are now about leveraging your social networks, engaging with people online and educating.

This is, essentially, the social sales model:

PAST	PRESENT	FUTURE
Employees	Role Models	Ambassadors
Cold Calls	Tribes	Engagement
Sales Demonstrations	Education	Thought Leadership
Salesperson	Trusted Adviser	Expert
Transaction	Solution Selling	Lifetime Partnership

Today, the businesses and entrepreneurs that make the most impact on their audiences are role models. They're trusted advisers who create tribes – powerful online communities that help their brands grow. They educate and provide solutions. They've jumped on board the social sales train and have embraced the connection economy whole-heartedly. Because if you don't embrace change, you get left behind.

But, as leaders, we can't rest on our laurels. We must build on this massive sales reform and look to the future. We must become trusted industry ambassadors; thought leaders who engage meaningfully with our followers, share generously our expertise and regard our audiences not just as leads or dollar signs, but as lifetime partnerships.

Impact for experts

Solopreneurs are the way of the future. They account for 61% of Australian businesses[31] And with the advent of freelance sites such as Upwork, 99designs, Freelancer and Airtasker, an increasing number of Australians are freelancing. According to freelance marketplace Elance-o Desk, 30% of the Australian workforce—or 3.7 million people— undertake some form of freelance work[32].

Digital marketing presents an enormous opportunity for solopreneurs. According to the Ipsos Open Thinking Exchange, the average person spends two hours a day on the internet. Furthermore, IBM's Global CEO Study found that CEOs believe social media utilisation for customer engagement will increase by 256% over five years. This means social media will become the second-most popular way to engage customers after face-to-face communication.

Social media has created a level playing field. It's cheap and readily available. You don't need large amounts of money to build a solo business. You don't even need an existing client base—you can start one online from scratch. The internet has given **everyone** the potential to create a successful solo business.

But there's a downside to this equal opportunity. Despite the accessibility of social media, one of the biggest challenges entrepreneurs and leaders continue to face is finding and retaining clients and talent.

The digital marketplace means you're competing against everyone else with a business like yours. You can't simply create a LinkedIn or Facebook account and expect clients to come to you. How will they know you're there? What makes you stand out? When everyone else is pushing their unique selling point, what will make people choose you?

In a world where customers have immediate access to information on every kind of business around the world, it's hard to cut through the noise. To gain that competitive edge, you must create a connection. You need to educate, lead and gain trust.

"If people like you, they'll listen to you, but if they trust you, they'll do business with you."

– Zig Ziglar

As a result of all this reasoning and why it matters, it's time to consider how to create a shift and increase trust as a leader. There is only one of you, and while it may seem you can't create a big enough change in the world, you can have control over the activities that build trust in you as a leader.

The three key areas of trust are:

1. Authenticity. The ability to be the best, most real version of you. This includes a self-awareness of your strengths, weaknesses and how you communicate with others to create connection and respect at a human level.

2. Empathy. The ability to gain an insight and understanding of others. You understand their experiences, pain points and aspirations. You think of creative ways to engage, collaborate and connect with people to create greater influence.

3. Credibility. The ability to manage your time and resources to get results. Are you able to help people achieve what they want to achieve? Have you got the runs on the board and are you able to gain respect from others to create influence?

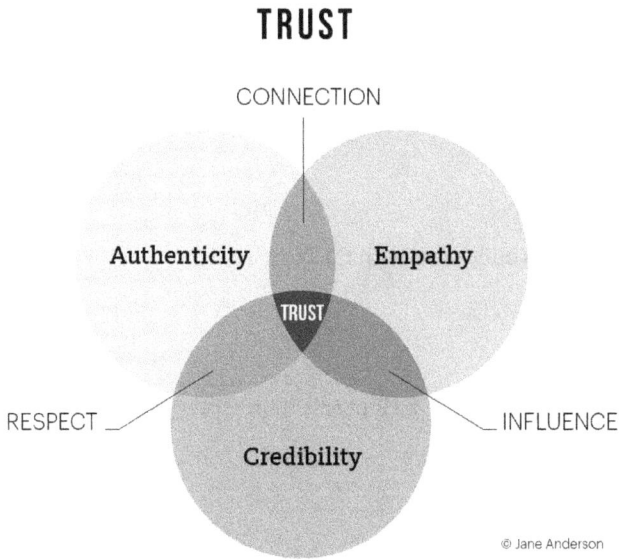

TRUST

CONNECTION

Authenticity

Empathy

TRUST

RESPECT

Credibility

INFLUENCE

© Jane Anderson

QUESTIONS

1. Why does trust matter to you?

2. How do you know if people trust you?

3. Whom do you build trust with the most easily?

4. What would the impact be if people didn't trust you?

5. How well trusted is your profession?

6. What strategies do you find work best to build trust in your industry?

7. What can you foresee in the future that may impact on building trust with your customers?

NOTES

[1] Barbara Brooks Kimmel, "Which countries are the most trustworthy?" The FCPA Blog, October 17, 2018. http://www.fcpablog.com/blog/2018/10/17/which-countries-are-the-most-trustworthy.html

[2] "2018 Country Trust Index™ Rankings", Trust Across America – Trust Around the World. https://trustacrossamerica.com/documents/reports/Country-Trust-Index-Rankings-2018.pdf

[3] Barbara Brooks Kimmel, "Which countries are the most trustworthy?" The FCPA Blog, October 17, 2018. http://www.fcpablog.com/blog/2018/10/17/which-countries-are-the-most-trustworthy.html

[4] Bill McEvily and Marco Tortoriello, "Measuring trust in organisational research: Review and recommendations," Journal of Trust Research, Volume 1, Issue 1, April 12, 2011. https://www.tandfonline.com/doi/abs/10.1080/21515581.2011.552424

[5] "Roy Morgan Image of Professions Survey 2017: Health professionals continue domination with Nurses most highly regarded again; followed by Doctors and Pharmacists," Roy Morgan, June 7, 2017. http://www.roymorgan.com/findings/7244-roy-morgan-image-of-professions-may-2017-201706051543

[6] "ALDI, Bunnings, Qantas and ABC the Most Trusted Brands in Australia," Roy Morgan, August 27, 2018. http://www.roymorgan.com/findings/7709-roy-morgan-annual-net-trust-score-review-august-2018-201808272319

[7] Mina Martin, "Australia 'unsophisticated' on cyber – industry expert," Insurance Business Australia, May 2, 2017. https://www.insurancebusinessmag.com/au/news/breaking-news/australia-unsophisticated-on-cyber-industry-expert-66442.aspx

[8] James Eyers, "ABA looks to code of conduct to restore public's trust in banks," Financial Review, August 27, 2017. https://www.afr.com/business/banking-and-finance/aba-looks-to-code-of-conduct-to-restore-publics-trust-in-banks-20170827-gy4yuw

[9] Jessica Irvine, Sarah Danckert and Clancy Yeates, "'Just appalling': AMP misconduct and lies exposed," The Sydney Morning Herald, April 17, 2018. https://www.smh.com.au/business/banking-and-finance/just-appalling-amp-misconduct-and-lies-exposed-20180417-p4za67.html

[10] Sarah Danckert, "CBA charged client fees for 10 years after death," The Sydney Morning Herald, April 19, 2018. https://www.smh.com.au/business/banking-and-finance/cba-charged-client-fees-for-10-years-after-death-20180419-p4zag1.html

[11] Clancy Yeates and Ruth Williams, "Brenner's position still 'in question', say AMP investors," The Sydney Morning Herald, April 20, 2018. https://www.smh.com.au/business/banking-and-finance/brenner-s-position-still-in-question-say-amp-investors-20180420-p4za01.html

[12] Rachel Clun, "How Scott Morrison changed his tune on the banking royal commission," The Sydney Morning Herald, April 20, 2018. https://www.smh.com.au/politics/federal/how-scott-morrison-changed-his-tune-on-the-banking-royal-commission-20180420-p4za0a.html

[13] Sarah Danckert, "'Economic self-harm': Morrison cautions against bank break-ups," The Sydney Morning Herald, April 20, 2018. https://www.smh.com.au/business/banking-and-finance/economic-self-harm-morrison-cautions-against-bank-break-ups-20180420-p4zann.html

[14] "ALDI, Bunnings, Qantas and ABC the Most Trusted Brands in Australia," Roy Morgan, August 27, 2018. http://www.roymorgan.com/findings/7709-roy-morgan-annual-net-trust-score-review-august-2018-201808272319

[15] Patrick Hatch, "Dreamworld tragedy: Ardent chairman Neil Balnaves defends CEO Deborah Thomas' bonus," The Sydney Morning Herald, October 27, 2016. https://www.smh.com.au/business/dreamworld-boss-asks-for-time-while-authorities-establish-the-facts-20161027-gsbopn.html

[16] Pamela S. Shockley-Zalabak, Sherwyn Morreale and Michael Hackman, Building the High-Trust Organization: Strategies for Supporting Five Key Dimensions of Trust, Jossey-Bass, 2010.

[17] Stephen Covey, "The Business Case for Trust," Chief Executive, June 4, 2007. https://chiefexecutive.net/the-business-case-for-trust/

[18] Ty Kiisel, "Who Do You Trust?" Forbes, June 13, 2012. https://www.forbes.com/sites/tykiisel/2012/06/13/who-do-you-trust/#31411d3c4789

[19] Sean Murray, "The Economic Value of Trust," RealTime Performance, June 30, 2009.

[20] Stephen R. Covey, First Things First, Free Press, 1996.

[21] Jessica Pryce-Jones, Happiness at Work: Maximizing Your Psychological Capital for Success, Wiley, 2010.

[22] Ryan General 2018, 'How an Alibaba Receptionist Became One of the Company's Top Executives', Nextshark 2018, https://nextshark.com/tong-wenhong-alibaba-receptionist/ (accessed 18 January 2018)

[23] "The Top Issues CEOs Face These Days," The Wall Street Journal, March 19, 2014. https://www.wsj.com/articles/executive-leadership-what-are-the-top-issues-ceos-face-these-days-1395267060

[24] "Future of Work 2030," PwC, May 2018. https://www.pwc.nl/nl/dienstverlening/people-and-organisation/documents/pwc-future-of-work-2030.pdf

[25] "CEOs cite reputational and brand risk as a top current concern," KPMG, June 14, 2017. https://home.kpmg/sk/en/home/media/press-releases/2017/06/ceo-cite-reputational-and-brand-risk-as-top-concern.html

[26] "How leaders can earn the trust of employees," HRD: Human Resources Director Australia, June 7, 2017. https://www.hcamag.com/hr-news/how-leaders-can-earn-the-trust-of-employees-235912.aspx

[27] Jenna Goudreau, "The 2 Things People Judge You on Immediately, According to a Harvard Psychologist," Money, December 28, 2018.

[28] Holly Henderson Brower, Scott Wayne Lester and M. Audrey Korsgaard. "Want Your Employees to Trust You? Show You Trust Them," Harvard Business Review, July 5, 2017.

[29] "The Bottom Line on Trust," Accenture, October 30, 2018.

[30] "5 Non-Obvious Trends Changing Business In 2019," Rohit Bhargava, December 7, 2018. https://www.rohitbhargava.com/2018/12/2019-non-obvious-trends-sneak-preview.html

[31] Australian Bureau of Statistics, June 2014

[32] Elance-o Desk survey, 2015

Can You Measure Trust?

"Trust is the highest form of
human motivation."

– Stephen Covey

According to one of the world's leading researchers on management and organisational trust, Joanna Paliszkiewicz, there are more than 120 different types of assessments that can identify your ability to build trust.[1] I suggest you choose one that feels most relevant to you and raises your level of self-awareness. It's not until we are asked meaningful questions that we truly get to explore our untapped potential to create a deeper, more powerful connection with those we work with and lead.

Here is a simple tool you can use, based on the contents of this book, to identify your ability to build trust in your team or tribe. The Trusted Leadership Index is a series of statements designed to give you an insight into your level of trust. Try not to overthink the statements or your response to them.

Trusted Leadership Index (TLI)

Give yourself a score of one out of three for each, with one being the lowest (you least agree) and three being the highest (you most agree).

Add your scores to find out where you are on the trust-building scale and what actions you should focus on next.

QUESTION	SCORE
1. Identity	
a. I am aware of my values—what drives and motivates me as a person and leader.	
b. I take time to reflect on my strengths and weaknesses.	
c. I am comfortable in my own skin and don't compare myself to others.	
2. Authenticity	
a. I feel comfortable being myself.	
b. I have a tribe of people around me who love me for who I am.	
c. I am not afraid for people to see the real me.	
3. Credibility	
a. I allocate time in my calendar to get work done.	
b. I meet deadlines, tasks and projects.	
c. I receive referrals regularly.	
4. Vulnerability	
a. I am not afraid to discuss my failures.	
b. I share personal stories to help others grow.	
c. I am not embarrassed or ashamed to share my journey.	

5. Empathy		
	a. I notice when others are experiencing challenges and take action to support or help them.	
	b. When influencing others, I can identify their specific challenges and connect them to my idea or solution.	
	c. I listen and ask questions more than I speak.	
6. Advocacy		
	a. I am not afraid to speak up on behalf of others.	
	b. I check in to ensure people are heard and have a chance to contribute.	
	c. I encourage others to engage with people who are not voicing their opinions to ensure everyone is heard.	
7. Humility		
	a. I ask others for feedback and input into my personal and career growth.	
	b. I am accepting and non-judgmental of others.	
	c. I am comfortable apologising to others, even if they are my subordinates.	
8. Inclusivity		
	a. I take active steps to create a diverse tribe of people from a variety of backgrounds of age, gender and race.	
	b. I create a culture of connection in our tribe and create opportunities for people to undertake technical and personal growth.	
	c. I take proactive steps to teach others how to create a culture of inclusivity in our tribe.	

9. Transparency	
a. I am comfortable giving direct, ethical honest and open feedback.	
b. I am confident in the steps I need to take when challenged with ethical decisions for myself or my tribe.	
c. I proactively teach others how to manage their ethical decision-making so they lead effectively in their role.	
TOTAL SCORE	**/ 81**

If you scored 0-27

It's time to think about the impact low trust is having in your team or tribe. Perhaps you're struggling to get people to be open with you. Are they sitting back, waiting to be heard? Are they holding on to past experiences and stories that may not be of service to them or you? A great way to start turning this around is to ask questions. Engage your team and listen to their needs. Think about implementing some of the activities in this book to build people's trust in you.

If you scored 28-54

Well done, you're on the right track! You're aware of the impact of your level of trust in your team/tribe. Now you must learn the specific actions that will amplify and sustain your trust in the future. Consider implementing some projects or new habits and routines to build trust in your tribe and create a safe space for people to undertake transformational growth.

If you scored 55-81:

Wow, great work! You not only build trust with your team/tribe, but you also teach others how to build trust. Consider ways you can coach the people around you and ask them questions about how they can build trust in their teams and tribes. Consider becoming a trust champion in your organisation.

NOTES

[1]   Joanna   Paliszkiewicz,   "Inter-Organizational   Trust: Conceptualization   and   Measurement,"
International Journal of Performance Measurement, 2011, Vol. 1, 15-28. https://pdfs.semanticscholar.
org/22af/45ebc0564fa32391edb8264418745363c0cd.pdf

How to
Build Trust

CHAPTER THREE

"Trust is hard to come by. That's why
my circle is small and tight. I'm kind
of funny about making new friends."

– Eminem

Your personal brand as a leader builds trust and creates your legacy.

According to **Forbes**, **trust affects a leader's impact** and the company's bottom line more than any other factor.[1] There is no better example of this than in 2018, when Johnathan Thurston (or, as he is affectionately known, JT), captain of the North Queensland Cowboys, an Australian rugby league football team, played his final game of professional football. JT had received a series of knockbacks at the beginning of his career from clubs that said he was too small to play in the National Rugby League (NRL). Thurston was eventually given his chance by the Canterbury Bulldogs, which handed the then 19-year-old his top-grade debut in round 13 of the 2002 season, albeit an unpaid position. He moved to the Cowboys in 2005 and went on to become arguably one of the greatest NRL players of all time. As you will see in this chapter, Thurston created a powerful identity and reputation built on trust and authenticity, both in and out of the game.

One of the biggest mistakes a leader can make is to think their role or position automatically means they have trust. Trust does not come from a title alone. It comes from dedication, patience, commitment and hard work. On occasion, it may mean having to prove yourself more than usual so others believe you can do the job.

Author and business expert Stephen Covey once said, "When the trust account is high, communication is easy." When you have trust, you build relationships, lead change, gain results faster and attract and retain great talent. A lack of trust lowers productivity, morale and reputation.

At a high level, gaining trust comes from three areas: **authenticity, empathy and credibility.** Once you integrate these three aspects into your character and communication, you increase connection, influence and respect—all of which are critical to leading teams through times of dramatic disruption and change.

1. Identity

In 2008, Thurston was selected for the Indigenous All Stars, the NRL's Aboriginal and Torres Strait Islander team, for the first time. This prompted him to learn more about his Aboriginal culture, and he began to carve a deeper sense of self and identity. He said the time he spent with tribal elders and people from his indigenous community resulted in the stories he shared off the field to lead, educate, inspire and bring out the best in others.

When you have a strong sense of identity, you have a clarity of purpose, vision and a way forward. Our identity or DNA is formed long before we're born. It is powerful in shaping who we become later in life.

Professor Jeffrey Jensen Arnett, an expert in early adolescence, says in his

9 PILLARS OF THE TRUSTED LEADER

—————————— T R U S T ——————————

ME	YOU	WE
3 Productivity	**6** Connection	**9** Truth
CREDIBILITY	VULNERABILITY	TRANSPARENCY
Control	Shame	Fear
2 Genuine	**5** Understanding	**8** Respect
AUTHENTICITY	EMPATHY	INCLUSIVITY
Manipulation	Assumptions	Status
1 Clarity	**4** Voice	**7** Safety
IDENTITY	ADVOCACY	HUMILITY
Validation	Self-serving	Ego

CONNECTION

© Jane Anderson

book **Adolescence and Emerging Adulthood**[2] that despite the fact most countries legally recognise a person as an adult at 18 years of age, people now don't develop behaviourally and neurologically into adulthood until age 30. This is due to many factors. In the past, our options were limited: finish school, go to university, get a job, get married, buy a home, have children. Today, we have so many options for what to do with our lives. This means it takes us much longer to develop our sense of identity and become our most congruent selves.

Arnett says getting married is a life experience that commonly helps people establish their sense of identity. In JT's case, his search for identity and need to spend time learning about his culture were precursors to him marrying his wife, which further solidified his sense of self.

Reid Hoffman, the founder of LinkedIn, once said, *"You remake yourself as you grow and as the world changes. Your identity doesn't get found. It emerges."*

2. Authenticity

JT was a gifted player, but the journey he took to learn more about his identity was what created a sense of authenticity about who he was.

When your authenticity is high, people perceive you as being genuine. This reduces their fear of manipulation and they are more likely to feel safe around you.

When people build a business, network or friendships, they look for people who are genuine. After all, nobody wants to work or hang out with a phony. It's essential you surround yourself with people who are genuine. And you must be genuine, too.

Being genuine is a rare quality. In a world full of fads, media hype and virtual personas, where everyone wants what they don't have, nobody's content to be who they are and, most importantly, nobody's willing to admit it—genuineness is becoming rarer all the time.

Several traits can help you determine whether someone is genuine. Some of them include:

• **They don't need attention.** They are self-confident and self-aware.

• **They don't need to be liked.** They forge their own path and are themselves. They don't need to manipulate people into liking them.

• **They can identify inauthentic people.** They are grounded and can tell when someone is trying to fool them or when things don't add up.

• **They're happy within themselves.** They don't need a lot of material possessions. They find happiness and fulfilment in their friends, family and interests, and are grateful for them.

• **They don't exaggerate.** They don't stretch the truth or sugar-coat things. They're direct and honest and say what needs to be said without bragging.

• **They're thick-skinned.** They don't take things personally and aren't easily offended.

3. Credibility

When JT started his rugby league career, many clubs wouldn't take him on due to his small size. He worked hard and eventually took on an unpaid position at the Bulldogs in 2002. The club didn't trust he had the goods, so he had a lot to prove. It wasn't a challenge he took lightly.

To build credibility, you need a strong sense of personal responsibility. It's up to you to show others your strengths. And, as a leader, it's not always about what happens to *you*, it's about what happens *next*.

Since those early days and knockbacks, not only did JT play 303 games and become known as the hardest worker on and off the field, in his 17-year career, he accumulated numerous awards, including:

• 2018: Queensland Australian of the Year

• 2017: Australian Human Rights Medal

• Two premierships

• **Dally M Medal Player of the Year:** 2005, 2007, 2014, 2015

• **Dally M Halfback of the Year:** 2005, 2007, 2009, 2015

• **Dally M Five-Eighth of the Year:** 2012, 2013, 2014

• **Dally M Captain of the Year:** 2015

• **RLPA Player of the Year:** 2005, 2013, 2014, 2015

• **RLIF International Back of the Year:** 2007

• **RLIF Halfback of the Year:** 2009, 2011, 2015

- **Rugby League World Golden Boot Award:** 2011, 2013, 2015

- **Rugby League Week Player of the Year:** 2007

- **Indigenous Halfback of the Century:** 1908-2007

- **North Queensland Cowboys Player of the Year:** 2005, 2012, 2014, 2015

- **North Queensland Cowboys Players' player of the Year:** 2011, 2014

- **Provan-Summons Medal:** 2014, 2015

- **Clive Churchill Medal:** 2015

- **Alan Clarkson Trophy:** 2015

- **Graham Murray Medal:** 2016

- **Arthur Beetson Medal:** 2017

- **Wally Lewis Medal:** 2008

- **Ron McAuliffe Medal:** 2012

- **Preston Campbell Medal:** 2010, 2017

- **Ken Stephen Medal:** 2012

- **Australian Representative Player of the Year:** 2014

- **2013 Rugby League World Cup Man of the Match awards** in the four games he played

- **State of Origin Man of the Match:** Five awards

- **State of Origin most consecutive matches:** 36 (2005-2016)

- **State of Origin all-time highest point scorer**

- **Townsville Bulletin Fan Choice Award:** 2014, 2015

With such credibility, it's no wonder JT commanded so much respect and influence in the industry and community. Credibility is gained through consistency. In Thurston's case, his credibility was the result of consistently performing to an exceptionally high standard.

In addition to consistency, there are several ways you can gain credibility:

• **Be sincere.** Sincerity means refraining from saying everything you think but meaning everything you say. You can't claim it; you must be it. Sincerity requires commitment, dedication and the willingness to be steadfast, unmovable and straightforward, no matter what.

• **Be respectful.** Treat everyone with respect—not because you expect something in return but because people deserve it. Titles are granted, positions are given, but showing respect is what earns you credibility.

• **Be loyal.** Your credibility grows when you act out of the best interests of those around you. It's about serving and protecting others. Loyalty creates a mutual commitment to success.

• **Be accountable.** Take responsibility for your decisions and actions. When you make a mistake, own up to it and take steps to correct it. When you aren't sure about something, say so.

• **Be principled.** Stop comparing yourself to others and learn to be yourself. Stand by your values. Serve those around you with your unique conviction and always strive to be better than you were yesterday.

We'll explore a few of these principles and more in greater detail in this book.

4. Curiosity

In his quest to improve his skills and be the best, Thurston constantly sought advice from mentors and experts. He wasn't afraid to explore new ideas and options.

Without curiosity, our performance stagnates. We continue to focus on the status quo and, as a result, we lose sight of what is happening. By tapping into the expertise of others, JT increased his ability to problem-solve under pressure and be in almost any part of the field at any moment during the game.

5. Vulnerability

When JT won the Dally M in 2015, he broke down when talking about his family's support. He was open about the struggles he went through with his wife Samantha to have children. It was clear their challenges were what made their bond with each other and their children so special. Over the years, JT fought back the tears in many award ceremonies and interviews, overcome with emotion when acknowledged for his performance as a rugby league player and community leader.

Vulnerability creates a powerful connection with others. It demonstrates you're real and unafraid of what others could perceive as shame. Being vulnerable also permits others to be vulnerable, creating a safe environment for them to make mistakes.

If you aren't vulnerable, if you advocate perfectionism and pretend to be perfect, you repel and alienate people. Often, the most impactful opportunities to build trust and strengthen your team arise when things aren't working. Successfully communicating those opportunities and supporting each other as teammates will increase others' confidence in you as a leader.

Other ways to become more vulnerable in your leadership include:

• **Asking for help.** Putting your hand up for help isn't always easy, especially if you're the one to always help others. Asking for help is a level of surrender, which can be hard if you've always been in charge. However, the best leaders know when they need help, advice, guidance or support. It's what makes them so powerful and effective. The key is to accept help when it's offered. There's no shame in receiving support. It honours the person providing it as they feel they have been able to do something positive.

• **Sharing your faults.** We're not all perfect and there's no point pretending to be, but sharing your flaws helps create a deep connection. It shows authenticity and humility and builds trust. Admitting to your mistakes also increases respect as you "walk the talk" and don't just pay lip service to how to behave.

• **Challenging your self-doubts.** We all have times where we question our value, knowledge or abilities. Rather than let them take over and run on autopilot, find ways to challenge them. A great way to do this is to tap into the close members of your tribe (trusted friends, mentors and advisors) who can help you to see if your doubts are real or imagined and how to regain some perspective.

As Brene Brown says, *"Vulnerability is the birthplace of innovation, creativity and change."*

6. Empathy

Towards the end of the 2015 NRL grand final, Brisbane Broncos player Ben Hunt dropped the ball and effectively lost the game for his team. After the game, Hunt was bitterly disappointed. The Cowboys had won their maiden NRL title after Thurston kicked a golden-point field goal to beat the Brisbane Broncos 17-16.

Thurston sought out Hunt for a few quiet words. "I didn't want him to feel the loss of the game was on his shoulders," he said. "He was outstanding for that 80 minutes and really controlled the game from a Bronco's point of view, so I just told him to hold his head up high."[3]

JT was known to reach out to players at other clubs who were going through a tough time. Whether they'd had a bad game, got into trouble or were suffering an injury, he understood he had a responsibility as a leader not just in his club, but for people in other clubs as human beings, mates and friends.

Empathy is one of the most influential traits you can have as a leader. It is the ability to understand how others might be feeling. The ability to remove assumptions and truly connect with what others are going through creates a human experience that's difficult for any machine or artificial intelligence to replicate.

In the following chapters, we'll explore ways you can increase and demonstrate empathy to build greater trust. Some of these behaviours include:

• **Putting aside your viewpoint.** There's nothing worse than trying to communicate with someone who is close-minded, stubborn and unreasonable. The ability to maintain your own beliefs while still being understanding of others, even if you don't agree with them, shows great empathy.

• **Looking at your attitude.** Being aware of your thoughts, judgements and decisions about others can be helpful. Ensuring your ego is in check and forgoing the need to always be right are valuable in connecting with others and showing empathy.

• **Encouraging people.** Taking the time to support and inspire is critical to create connection and ensure the growth of others. Of course, encouragement must be authentic and relevant with the aim of creating genuine outcomes.

• **Listening.** Truly listening without being distracted or wanting to jump in can take real practice. Being present is key and paying attention with all parts of your body is essential. You can do this by:

• *Listening with your ears:* What tone, keywords and phrases are used? Does the person repeat particular words? What is the first word they say when responding to a question?

• *Listening with your eyes:* How is the person saying what they are saying?

• *Listening with your instincts:* What is the person not saying?

In the words of poet Maya Angelou, *"I think we all have empathy. We may not have enough courage to display it."*

7. Humility

JT surrounded himself with leaders and continuously asked the question, "How can I be better?" He credits past players and his wife for their support and role in his success. When the Bulldogs won the 2003 premiership, he gave his premiership ring to the captain, Steve Price, who was out injured, forming a bond that would last a lifetime.

A leader's ability to remove their ego creates a greater sense of openness. It provides others with a safe platform to share and be vulnerable.

One of the most important human characteristics is humility. Yet, most of us fail to show it. We're often the opposite. We brag and we boast. We take pictures and do things so we can display a public persona to the world. However, what most people don't realise is that many can see right through this facade.

Humility is the opposite of hubris. It is the quality or state of being humble.[4] It involves suppressing the desire to shine a spotlight on yourself and the good deeds you're doing. It involves removing pride and having the emotional fortitude and spiritual capacity not to showcase, brag or boast.

In fact, studies have linked humility to better job performance[5] and generosity.[6] People who are humble are more positively perceived and recognised as being less deceptive in their social interactions, as well.

As author C.S. Lewis said, *"True humility is not thinking less of yourself, it's thinking of yourself less."*

8. Inclusivity

One of JT's qualities was his ability to make people feel special. A feature of his game was to acknowledge the children in the crowd. He would do this by personally handing the kicking tee to the young ball boy and donating his signature protective headgear to a young fan in the crowd after every game. He also stayed behind to sign autographs, often to the frustration of waiting media outlets.

When you act out of a sense of equality, you tell others you respect them. The law of reciprocity kicks in and you create greater respect for yourself.

Inclusivity gives everyone an opportunity to contribute. It allows the discussion of divergent perspectives and approaches. It also reduces the focus on status and puts greater emphasis on human connection.

Businesses are increasingly realising the value of this. As many as 150 CEOs from some of the largest companies in the US have publicly committed to diversity and inclusion efforts, pledging to "foster more open discussion about race and gender in the workplace."[7] Hiring, compensation and promotion practices are under scrutiny, and many companies are scrambling to get ahead of this issue before they become tomorrow's headline.

Here are some ways you can be more inclusive in your workplace, team or tribe, which we'll explore in greater detail later in this book:

• **Bounce an idea off someone unexpected.** If you work in the marketing team, chances are you've not worked with any of the team in procurement, for example. Finding ways to collaborate and connect across functions can drive innovation and growth by removing group-think and fostering a more egalitarian culture.

• **Remove assumptions.** It is easy and often natural to make assumptions about others in the workplace. The problem is, this leads to misunderstandings, biases and wrong conclusions. The next time you find yourself making an assumption about someone, even if it's as simple as, "She's probably too busy," stop yourself. Ask the individual first. Even if you assumed correctly, at least you've given the person the opportunity to be involved and they know you have considered them.

• **Find out more about others' interests outside of work.** It can be amazing how much common ground we have with people when we take the time to find out about their interests outside of work. Finding out about their family, where they grew up, or their favourite sport builds a stronger connection. Being curious to connect and learn creates a culture of respect and trust in our teams and tribes.

The topic of inclusion can be broad and intimidating because it's not always clear what role individuals can play. But, as Steven Covey said, *"Strength lies in differences, not in similarities."*

9. Transparency

In 2010, Thurston was arrested and sent to the watch-house for disorderly behaviour. In a separate on-field incident, he verbally abused a referee. He publicly apologised and acknowledged these incidents were out of character and shouldn't have happened. Admitting to his faults, JT credited his wife for supporting him to get on the "straight and narrow" and telling him to clean up his act.

When we're transparent about our mistakes, we reduce the fear and anxiety of our stakeholders and team. They know what is going on and what you will do to fix the situation. Keeping people in the loop also increases a sense of safety as they no longer feel they must always second guess your words and actions and read between the lines.

Atlassian, one of the world's "best places to work", ranks transparency as one of its most important values. And according to TinyPulse, a business-to-business SaaS employee survey firm, transparency is **the top factor** that contributes to employee happiness.[8]

In a later chapter, we'll discuss some of the ways you can include greater transparency in your tribe, including honesty, sharing results, breaking down silos and the tools to support transparency.

What a remarkable career to date for JT! The best part was he left his rugby league career on an incredible high with the world as his oyster. His leadership and ability to share his personal growth journey are what makes him so real, relatable and a role model. I'll be watching him intently as he still has a lifetime ahead of him, being only 35.

When you reach the end of your career, what would you like people to say about you?

QUESTIONS TO CONSIDER

1. **Identity.** *What is your personal brand, history and where do you come from?*

2. **Authenticity.** *Are you surrounded by people who encourage you to be the best version of you?*

3. **Credibility.** *Do you do the work or only say you do the work?*

4. **Curiosity.** *How often and to whom do you reach out to for feedback? Do you listen to the right people?*

5. **Vulnerability.** *How often do you allow people to see the parts of you that may not appear perfect?*

6. **Empathy.** *When was the last time you reached out to someone who was suffering and shared your challenges to support and encourage them?*

7. **Humility.** *Do you acknowledge others for their successes?*

8. **Equality.** *How often do you connect with others who may not be as senior as you and see you as a role model?*

9. **Transparency.** *Do you apologise when you make a mistake?*

NOTES

[1] David Horsager, "You Can't Be A Great Leader Without Trust – Here's How You Build It," Forbes, October 24, 2012, https://www.forbes.com/sites/forbesleadershipforum/2012/10/24/you-cant-be-a-great-leader-without-trust-heres-how-you-build-it/#6ff34ab4ef7a

[2] Jeffrey Jensen Arnett, Adolescence and Emerging Adulthood, Pearson, July 12, 2012

[3] Andrew Dickson, "NRL grand final: Johnathan Thurston tells Bronco Ben Hunt to 'hold his head up high,'" ABC News, October 6, 2015. https://www.abc.net.au/news/2015-10-05/thurston-urged-disappointed-hunt-to-hold-his-head-up-high/6829186

[4] Merriam-Webster. https://www.merriam-webster.com/dictionary/humility

[5] "New Baylor Study Shows Higher Job Performance Linked to People Who are More Honest and Humble," Baylor, March 1, 2011. https://www.baylor.edu/mediacommunications/news.php?action=story&story=89350

[6] Julie J. Exline and Peter C. Hill, "Humility: A consistent and robust predictor of generosity," The Journal of Positive Psychology, March 27, 2012. https://www.tandfonline.com/doi/abs/10.1080/17439760.2012.671348

[7] CEO Action for Diversity & Inclusion. https://www.ceoaction.com/ceos/

[8] 2015 Employee Engagement Report, TINYpulse. https://www.tinypulse.com/lt-2015-employee-engagement-organizational-culture-report

CHAPTER FOUR

Identity |

"Identity is this incredible invisible
force that controls your whole life. It's
invisible, like gravity is invisible, but it
controls your whole life."

– *Tony Robbins*

If you haven't had the chance to see the movie **The Greatest Showman,** it's worth seeing.

Hugh Jackman plays circus founder and freak-show curator P.T. Barnum, who, in 1871, created what he called "The Greatest Show on Earth" by bringing together people who were ostracised from the community due to their physical appearance. Amazingly, the show ran for more than 80 years until it was sold to the Ringling brothers in 1909 to continue for another 108 years. What drove the show's ongoing success was the uniqueness of the cast members.

While this happened a long time ago, the theme of the story is relevant today. It can be difficult to celebrate our differences, particularly when society tells us what is normal. But if we were all the same, we would become commoditised and homogenised. Your uniqueness is what draws people to you. It's your edge, and it's like a magnet. You could say it's your personal power.

Don't get me wrong; your identity is not about being perfect. It's about being clear about who you are and who you're not.

As Al Ries, bestselling author of the classic marketing text Positioning: ***The Battle For Your Mind,*** says, "The essence of positioning is sacrifice. You must be willing to give up something in order to establish that unique position."

An example of this is when comedian Weird Al Yankovic declined to be in an ad for a beer company in the 1980s, even though it was prepared to pay him $5 million. He rejected the offer because his fans were young and impressionable. Yankovic understood that your identity is not just what you're known for but also what you don't want to be known for.

Giving up something to remain true to your uniqueness can be a challenge. You may have spent much of your time playing it safe, fitting in, not rocking the boat and keeping the peace. If this is the case, you haven't done yourself any favours. It's likely that everyone else is progressing because you have helped them, but you're still where you were this time last year.

Until you step into your light, everything stays the same. Only you can change that. Only you can amplify your value to your audience. P.T. Barnum isn't going to come past your desk and choose you for his circus. You must step into your power and create your own show. Everyone out there is trying to achieve their potential, so you might as well be the best version of you and attract those who value you the most.

Your personality, your lens and your experiences combine to create something others want to learn from you.

In this day and age of fast-moving change, its critical leaders are transparent.

Your identity matters. People want to know whom they're dealing with. They see through inauthenticity and they want the real deal. Trust is the currency and vulnerability and empathy are the keys to unlock it. The only way you can be vulnerable and empathetic as a leader is to humanise your identity and personal brand.

Business growth has changed

The following model shows why your identity and personal brand matter for business growth:

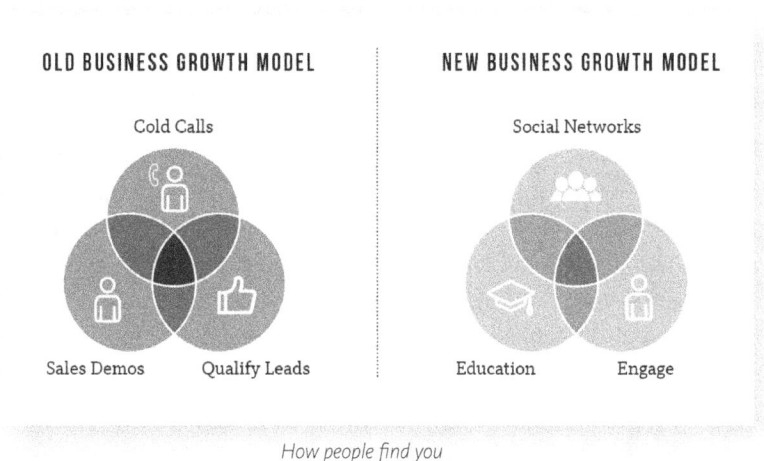

OLD BUSINESS GROWTH MODEL

Cold Calls

Sales Demos   Qualify Leads

NEW BUSINESS GROWTH MODEL

Social Networks

Education   Engage

How people find you

How people find you

When I first started working with my mentor, I thought, "Where on Earth have you been for the past four years?" I wished I'd known he existed much earlier. He had kept within his stream of clients and didn't do much social media marketing.

For a Generation Y/Xer like me, social media is where I hang out. It wasn't until someone who was being mentored by him reached out to have a coffee with me that I found out about him. This person told me about his mentor and I thought, "Wow, that's exactly what I'm after."

From a sales perspective, times have changed. We are in the era of the information superhighway. The challenge is that there is so much information and marketing material available. Unless you know what you need, it can be hard to know what do or where to turn. You either procrastinate, do nothing or buy what you think you need, then waste it because it wasn't what you were after. This is why cut-through is so crucial for businesses and leaders to connect with the right people.

How does your identity as a leader create cut-through for your team, tribe and potential clients?

Due to the oversupply of content, it's difficult for consumers to answer the age-old question: Who can help me solve this problem? My experience is that people typically do the following when they need help, whether they're aware of it or not.

The Tribe-Building for the New World of Business Model provides you with real, actionable steps to take you from expert to trusted leader and influencer. It will ensure that people not only find you but want to work with you. Each quadrant encompasses the digital space, social media, technology and new communication platforms, and the dynamics of each quadrant work quite differently. Positioning yourself as an influencer will allow you to dominate each quadrant with more ease, trust and growth.

TRIBE BUILDING

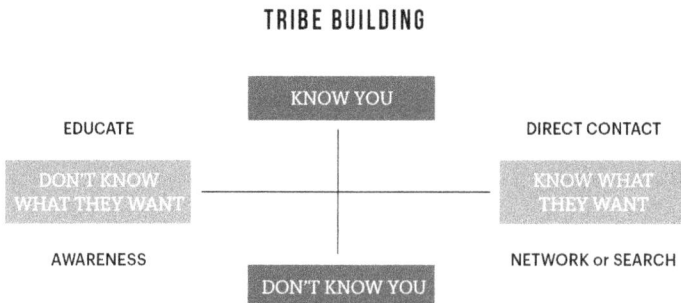

KNOW YOU

EDUCATE · DIRECT CONTACT

DON'T KNOW WHAT THEY WANT · KNOW WHAT THEY WANT

AWARENESS · NETWORK or SEARCH

DON'T KNOW YOU

© Jane Anderson

The model contains the following quadrants:

- **Direct Contact**
- **Network or Search**
- **Awareness**
- **Educate**

Each quadrant consists of three activities you must undertake to build your positioning as a trusted leader and influencer. The model also considers the four types of potential clients:

- People who know someone.

- People who know what they want.

- People who don't know someone.

- People who don't know what they want.

Let's examine these four types of consumers and how they relate to the different quadrants of the model.

Direct Contact

"I know someone who can help me and I know what I want."

This type of person already knows who you are. They know you offer what they need. But for people to take that next step and call or email you, you must be at the front of their mind. You will need to communicate with them regularly. Most leaders and influencers don't communicate enough and are afraid of annoying people, appearing "spammy" and thus, prompting people to unsubscribe. However, in the US, it's not unusual for influencers to communicate daily or at least three times per week via email.

A great example of someone who leverages direct contact effectively is Nikki Fogden-Moore, a vitality expert based on the Sunshine Coast in Queensland.

Nikki specialises in working with super-busy executives and entrepreneurs who are tired and lack energy and balance. Each Monday, she sends an email she calls her "Monday Mojo". It's a wonderful email to receive first thing each week and puts a spring in the receiver's step.

Building your connections database is critical to keeping in touch. Your database can include existing clients, people you've met or groups of people with a common interest or problem. You need to reach out to your database regularly to maintain visibility. The idea is that you come immediately to mind when they need you or when someone they know needs someone like you.

Direct contact is the most valuable quadrant of this model. Building your database requires plenty of groundwork and you must keep at it, day in, day out. The benefits are enormous. As Seth Godin says, "The people who will buy from you are those who know you."

Network or Search

"I don't know someone who can help me, but I know what I want."

In this situation, the potential client will seek recommendations. If they're extroverted or well-networked, they will consult their colleagues and friends for referrals, as they trust them. If they're introverted, they will conduct an online search. Sometimes, people do both.

Being referred by a network is ideal. It means you have a good reputation. And when you have a good reputation, you have solid positioning. It makes your job of finding new clients so much easier. Knowing who your current and potential key referrers are is crucial. Once you know who they are, you can apply specific strategies to reward and encourage them.

An excellent example of this is an insolvency firm we recently worked with. The field of financial planning, accounting and insolvency is complicated and requires a high level of knowledge, so the average consumer doesn't know what to do if their business becomes insolvent. Their first port of call will usually be a lawyer or accountant, who will then call an insolvency firm. Most business owners won't go directly to an insolvency agency, as it's so specialised. Essentially, insolvency firms are known for **knowing something.** They're influencers in their field. So, in your business or industry, you want to be like an insolvency firm: specialised, respected and easily referrable.

Being found on the top page of a Google search result is often considered to be the "nirvana" of business growth. For an influencer's practice, however, this isn't always the case. Usually, the potential client conducting the search doesn't know you. If no one has referred you to them, it's difficult for you to stand out. You'll be competing with all the other people and businesses that turn up in the search – some of whom may have extensive experience with search engine optimisation and Google AdWords. This means they may appear higher in the search results list than you, and the closer a business is to the top, the more likely the potential client will click on their link.

In a Google search, you look the same as everybody else – like toothpaste on a supermarket shelf. Selling your defining features in that space is difficult. You'll be competing on price, and that's an awkward space in which to sell. While your buyer may be ready, you need to be able to compete aggressively to stand out when you're found.

However, if you are well networked, your referrals will come to the fore – even in search engine results. If you don't have a LinkedIn profile, set one up now! Ultimately, LinkedIn is a search engine, so it's essential you set up your LinkedIn profile with the right keywords and include testimonials. That way, you'll be more likely to turn up in online search results.

Awareness

"I don't know someone who can help me and I don't know what I want."

This quadrant is about accessing new markets. People in new markets don't know you. They may not have come across your insights and they may not have even articulated the problems they have that you can solve. Ignorance can be bliss for customers in this quadrant, so you must penetrate the noise they're exposed to and grab their attention.

To engage this type of client, you need to build awareness. Let them know who you are, what you do, who you help and how you help. Blog posts, articles, videos, podcasts and social media profiles are all essential tools in your awareness arsenal.

The work you do offline is important, too. Public speaking, attending networking events and appearing at expos will help your potential clients get to know you. People will see that while they may not need your help right now, they might down the track—or someone they know will. The goal is to continually be proactive and reach out to others so you can grow your list and nurture them.

A great example of this is a client we recently worked with named Adam. Adam is an expert in creating high-performing schools and learning cultures. He's been so successful with this that he identified many corporate organisations had the same problems as schools. Adam could see they needed his help, so he decided to take his approach to the corporate market. In terms of getting clients, it was like starting his business all over again. So, we helped Adam access the people who didn't know him and who didn't know they had a problem he could solve. Adam had to be exceptionally proactive in reaching out to corporates and educating them about his message.

Advertising, public relations and radio are all valuable activities here, but in an influencer's world, your list is everything. It's so important you maximise every opportunity to build your list and nurture an awareness of what you do. You cannot simply live in the hope that the people on your list will need your help immediately because that's usually not the case.

Elon Musk is a fantastic example of someone who builds awareness exceptionally well. As the CEO of Tesla and SpaceX, he is renowned for going through PR consultants who don't immediately grasp his vision. He realises the value of raising the awareness of people who don't know him or his message of creating a sustainable planet.

Educate

"I know who can help me, but I don't know what I want."

Although they know who you are, these kinds of customers are not aware they need your help. In this case, it is your job to educate them. You must regularly create and share content so people understand what you do. By educating them on how you can help them, they may then realise they have a problem—they just weren't aware of it until now. People often don't understand they have an issue that needs resolving or an area they could improve on unless someone educates them.

Writing posts, sharing updates and providing insightful comments are simple ways to educate and demonstrate your deep understanding of the problems you solve. The goal of your content is to encourage your audience to think, "Wow, that's exactly what I'm after!" It must provide a clear connection between their problems and your solutions.

So, when building your identity as a trusted leader, you're asking yourself, "Who am I and what is my personal brand?"

What do you need to do from here to build your personal brand, position yourself as a trusted leader and get ready for the future? To consciously create your identity, you need to think about three key components:

1. Clarity

What is your background and where have you come from? The first step to gaining clarity is to get clear on your past. Where did you grow up, what are your values and what's important to you? What are your passions and strengths? What is your purpose?

Once you have considered your past, it's time to consider your future. What is it you want? What is your vision? Don't make employers, teams and customers guess, search or try to find it. Make it crystal clear for them with the words you use to describe yourself online.

BUILD A PERSONAL BRAND

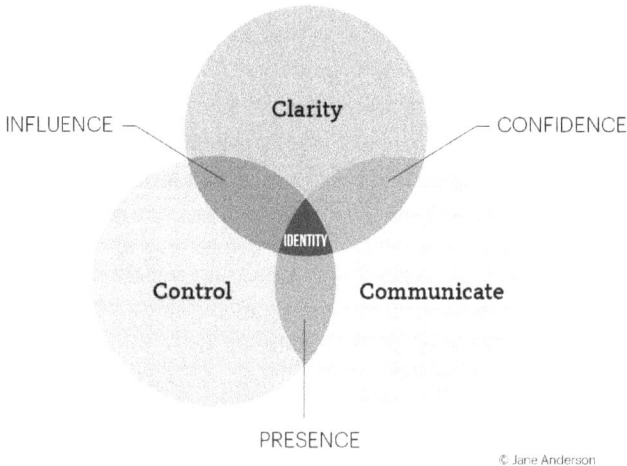

INFLUENCE — **Clarity** — CONFIDENCE

IDENTITY

Control **Communicate**

PRESENCE

© Jane Anderson

There is incredible power in writing your brand down. Sit down with your favourite notebook, laptop or tablet and articulate what kind of brand you want as a leader. Not only will this will help you process it; it will also allow your brand to morph, change and improve as you go through various drafts, making it even clearer for you. As a result, your brand will be well-defined for your audience.

2. Communication

You can't sell a secret! Think about where your ideal customer, recruiter, client, team member or thought leader hangs out. Is it on Facebook, Twitter or LinkedIn? Is it in the pub after work? If it's online, that's where you need to share your vision.

Make it clear to others what you want and be easy to find. Your connections will tell others that you're the person to talk to! Look at what your messages, posts and updates say. You need to "dress" for the positioning you want, not the positioning you've had. This may mean reframing your entire online presence into one that is more professional, streamlined and a better "fit" for the life you want to lead.

3. Control

Life deals us all sorts of curve balls. Inevitably, things go wrong at some point or another. Control is not about never making mistakes or never going through hard times. Control is about how you show up when things do go wrong—and they will. You're only human, and you can only do your best. So, be yourself when things go wrong and remember: it's not the end of the world. Tomorrow's another day, and hopefully, things will go better.

The fact is, we have more control and choice over things than we realise. By not taking control, we become resentful and unhappy as our circumstances may not align with our vision or the future we imagined. An ideal life is what you're trying to achieve in an aspirational sense, but it's not necessarily what you'll get.

Life isn't a straight line. Often, where we end up is better than where we imagined we'd be if only we looked at it objectively and saw things as opportunities rather than disappointments. Remember, as the saying goes, "You may not get to the moon, but you might reach the stars!" What have you done to take control of your identity and brand to achieve your dreams?

As Marianne Williamson said, *"Our deepest fear is not that we are inadequate. Our deepest fear is that we are powerful beyond measure. It is our light, not our darkness that most frightens us."*

Here are a few ways you can work on your identity and brand:

1. Find your tribe. Feeling alone, as though no one else is experiencing the same challenges, fears and setbacks, is hard. Take the time to find and build your tribe. Consider industry associations, Meetup groups or masterminds.

Being around like-minded people will allow you to feel more appreciated for your talents and will allow you to shine

2. Focus on your strengths. Instead of feeling like there's something wrong with you, consider what you're great at. What do you love doing and what would people pay you to do? This way, you will stay in your genius, work in flow and harness your energy into meaningful and fulfilling projects to grow your practice and career.

3. Play your own game. One of the surest ways to slow down is to compare yourself to others. In **The Greatest Showman,** Keala Settle plays the bearded lady who sings the emotive and touching song, "This is Me". There is a line in the song that says:

> *"Look out 'cause here I come*
> *And I'm marching on to the beat I drum*
> *I'm not scared to be seen*
> *I make no apologies, this is me."*

I find when working with clients on their positioning, they often feel raw, naked and vulnerable. It takes a lot of courage to be seen and stop hiding. The way around that is to stop looking at everybody else. Stay focussed on what you need to do and march to the beat of **your** drum.

4. Mind your self-talk. Michigan State University found that the average person has 80,000 thoughts per day and 80% of those thoughts are negative.[1] The impact of this is that our subconscious takes over and can't tell the difference between what is real and what isn't. The key is to catch yourself when you tell yourself, "I'm not good enough," and replace this thought with kind words as if you're your own best friend.

As another line in the song, "This is Me", goes:

> *"When the sharpest words wanna cut me down*
> *I'm gonna send a flood, gonna drown them out."*

Do you trust yourself?

In 2017, TIME magazine released profiles of the world's 100 most influential people. Jeff Bezos, the founder of Amazon, graced the cover. Each person featured was a celebrity or political figure, and the articles written about them were penned by other influencers. For example, philanthropist Melinda Gates' profile was written by Sheryl Sandberg, who described Melinda as "a fierce advocate for women around the world" whose "impact will be felt for generations."

The edition is undoubtedly inspiring, yet the challenge is that sometimes we see influencers like this and think, "What can I offer? How can I possibly make such an impact?"

And when I hear people – women in particular – say this, my thoughts are drawn to a special lady called Lillian Armfield.

Do you trust yourself?

In 2017, **TIME** magazine released profiles of the world's 100 most influential people.[2] Jeff Bezos, the founder of Amazon, graced the cover. Each person featured was a celebrity or political figure, and the articles written about them were penned by other influencers. For example, philanthropist Melinda Gates' profile was written by Sheryl Sandberg, who described Melinda as "a fierce advocate for women around the world" whose "impact will be felt for generations."

The edition is undoubtedly inspiring, yet the challenge is that sometimes we see influencers like this and think, "What can I offer? How can I possibly make such an impact?"

And when I hear people – women in particular – say this, my thoughts are drawn to a special lady called Lillian Armfield.

The story of Lillian Armfield

Lillian Armfield was born in 1884 at Mittagong, New South Wales, daughter of George Armfield, a labourer, and his wife, Elizabeth. Educated locally, Lillian was highly intelligent, well-schooled and had a good head for numbers.

Before her time

In 1907, Lillian became a nurse at the Hospital for the Insane in Callan Park, Sydney, where she looked after the female inmates. Due to her competence and kindness, in 1915, the medical superintendent recommended she apply for a newly established post as a police recruit in the NSW police force. At the time, there were no female police officers in Australia but this didn't deter her and she thought she would be well-suited to a career on the front line.

Lillian was successful in her application. In her starting role, she was paid the grand sum of 7 shillings, 6 pence a day. Unlike her male colleagues, Lillian's contract specified that no uniforms would be provided and no overtime or expenses allowed.

After a year's probation, she enrolled as a special constable. But her promotion came with a catch: Lillian was required to sign an agreement that subjected her to the same rules and discipline as her male colleagues but without the right to compensation for injuries received while performing her duties. In addition to this overt discrimination, Lillian was required to forego her right to superannuation and pension benefits.

Overseas interest

Lillian's appointment was watched with intense interest overseas, as she was the first plain-clothes female detective. So foreign was this concept of a female policewoman working alongside her male colleagues, it gained international attention.

In Paris, a captain for the French police declared that policewomen would be the subject of ridicule, prompting the following jingle in a Sydney newspaper:

"In gay Paree, no police you'll see parading around in skirts
For France prefers her mademoiselles as dainty, pretty flirts,
No Sergeant Armfield there you'll find, forever on the roam,
The French would jeer at women cops. They like their girls at home.

Oh ma Cherie, how sad 'twould be if Suzannes or Suzettes
Discarded silks and chic coiffures and scented cigarettes,
And turned to raiding restaurants and tracking thief and crook.
No longer caring what the world would wear or even cook."

The Trailblazer

Despite the ridicule, police from several American states asked for detailed reports of the experiment of a woman working as a plain-clothes police officer. And while Scotland Yard rebuked the idea of women working as plain-clothes detectives, it didn't rule them out of working in uniform.

Lillian's purpose was always to reclaim the women and girls who had turned to crime or fallen into the wrong crowd. Much of her time was spent encouraging runaway girls to return home before they encountered serious harm. This often led her to cases involving murder, rape, theft, drug-running and prostitution.

Although her contribution was praised and officially recognised, promotion throughout her 34-year career was slow. By November 1, 1923, Lillian had become a special sergeant, 3rd class, and by January 1, 1943, had risen to 1st class. In 1947, she received the King's Police and Fire Service Medal for outstanding service. After her retirement on December 2, 1949, aged 65, she was awarded the Imperial Service Medal in recognition of her contribution and service to the community.

At her funeral, NSW Police Commissioner N.T.W. Allan said, "She was a pioneer, a pathfinder for the present-day policewoman."

Her influence

What makes this story special and personal for me is that Lillian Armfield is my great aunt. Her legend and trailblazing exploits as Australia's first policewoman is a story not lost on my own family, five of whom are currently serving in various police roles across Australia.

Being one of three daughters, I can say Lillian's story has always inspired my sisters and me in our careers. No matter what career path we've pursued, we've always strived to balance kindness with the courage to serve our clients and have their best interests at heart.

To be an influencer, you don't have to be in **TIME** magazine or have thousands of followers on social media. It's not even about you. All that matters is who you influence and what impact you can make.

What's your story?

One of the most useful tools for building your personal brand is storytelling. The emotional connection it creates with your clients and leads is a marketing powerhouse. People often make decisions based on feelings and things that inspire them. Storytelling is the perfect platform to engage and move your audience and build their trust in you.

One of the best business stories I can think of is that of Don Meij, CEO of Domino's Pizza. Meij began his career in the pizza industry as a delivery driver for Silvio's Dial-A-Pizza in the 1980s. From this humble post, he steadily worked his way up the ranks and was promoted to general manager when Silvio's acquired Domino's Pizza in 1993. He then became a successful Domino's franchisee, building a network of 17 stores, which he sold in 2001. In 2002, he became Domino's CEO. He is, to this day, the face of Domino's Pizza.

Meij's story is so unique that people remember it. It's part of his personal brand. People like to barrack for the underdog; it's something most people can relate to and creates an emotional bond. You, too, can harness the power of storytelling to make an impact on your audience and establish your identity.

The first thing you need to do is understand your *why.* Why do you do what you do? As Simon Sinek, author of **Start With Why,** says, you need to feel inspired to inspire others. Understand your purpose and your passion, then infuse that passion into your storytelling. Bring it to life so others can tap into it and feel energised by it.

Storytelling can give you a distinct advantage over your competitors. It keeps you front of mind and encourages your audience to act. But you must be strategic with your storytelling. Yamini Naidu and Gabrielle Dolan, authors of **Hooked: How Leaders Can Engage and Inspire with Storytelling,** emphasise that your stories must have a strong message. What is the purpose of your story? What is your call to action? What do you want people to walk away with and what do you want them to do?

You may be thinking you have no stories to tell. The truth is, you are full of stories—you just need to record them! Keep a journal. Write down your thoughts or create a folder on your desktop and add to it regularly. Think about the obstacles you've faced and turning points in your career. What stories will engage your audience's hearts and minds so they'll want to work with you?

So many entrepreneurs shy away from storytelling because they don't want to be the centre of attention. I'm one of these people. It's not in my nature to be in the spotlight all the time. But I understand I need to put my reservations aside to make myself known. It's part of my job. I also need to do it to inspire my clients and help them feel at ease doing their presentations. When you have your identity and personal brand to build, you must learn to be comfortable with putting yourself and your why out there.

So, where should you tell your stories? In your keynote speeches and presentations, of course, but also in your blogs and podcasts. Social media posts and the "about us" page on your website are other great storytelling opportunities. Consider your message when deciding on your medium. Are you able to tell your story effectively in writing or would it have more impact if you delivered it verbally? To which platform would your target audience be more receptive?

You can read more about the art of storytelling in my book, **IMPACT: How to Build Your Personal Brand in the Connection Economy.**

QUESTIONS

1. What are your strengths?

2. If you had all the time and money in the world, what would you continue to do because you enjoy it so much?

3. What do you avoid spending your time on?

4. When does time seem to fly for you the most?

5. If you woke up in your ideal month, what would happen in that month? Who would you spend your time with? What would you work on?

6. What have been the most significant challenges in your life? What is the theme or recurring pattern?

7. Ask a group of 5-10 people what word comes to mind when they think of you. Even better, ask the question on Facebook and see what answers you get!

NOTES

[1] Maria Millett, "Challenge your negative thoughts," Michigan State University, March 31, 2017. https://www.canr.msu.edu/news/challenge_your_negative_thoughts

[2] "The 100 Most Influential People," TIME, 2017. http://time.com/collection/2017-time-100/

Authenticity |

"If I had known being authentic would
make me as rich as I've become, I would
have done it a long time ago."

– Oprah

One hot Sunday night in January 2017, I was fortunate enough to attend Adele's second sold-out concert in Brisbane. It was the city's biggest-ever concert, with more than 60,000 adoring fans packed into Brisbane's iconic sporting stadium, The Gabba. It's no wonder. The British superstar has sold millions of albums, won numerous Grammy awards and has one of the most powerful voices in the music industry.

Yet on stage, Adele is so down to earth. She's funny, genuine and authentic. She's entertainment royalty, world-class, yet people can easily relate to her.

Adele has the ideal personal brand. There are so many lessons we can learn from her as we build our trust and our own personally branded businesses.

Adele shows us that we can stand head and shoulders above the rest and still make genuine, meaningful connections with people.

But how does she do this?

1. She's instantly recognisable

Central to Adele's personal brand are her stunning eyes and trademark bold lashes. Adele likes to wear dramatic false eyelashes and thick eyeliner. At her concert, she appeared on stage with her eyes cast downwards. When the song "Hello" began, her eyes flicked open and the crowd roared with delight. It was something they immediately recognised.

2. She shows us she's human

Adele has an incredible sense of humour. Her infectious laugh[1] and her ability to poke fun at herself on stage makes her so human. Despite her light-hearted persona, many of her songs have a melancholic undertone. This is something she addresses on stage. This kind of personal interaction brings her even closer to her fans. She acknowledges her dark side, but can also lighten the mood when it's needed. Rather than automatically moving from song to song, she asks the audience questions: "How are you? Are you having a great time? Who received tickets tonight for their birthday?" This demonstrates she respects and cares about her fans, reinforcing her connection with them. Her comical reaction to some uninvited guests on stage—in this case, Brisbane's renowned subtropical insect life— drew laughs from the crowd and reinforced the fact she's only human.

3. She shares aspects of her life, interests and vulnerability

What came through in Adele's show was the love she has for her son. She talked about how he makes her world so special. She even took the time to make the children who were at the show feel included. Adele also revealed another—perhaps surprising—passion at her concert: basketball! Her own "kiss cam" – a live video feed during basketball and sporting events, where a camera scans the crowd and selects a couple who are encouraged by the audience to kiss—was a real hit. It was yet another insight into her sense of humour and "Adele the person".

Essentially, the key to Adele's effective personal brand is authentic communication. It's not all about her "genius"—her amazing singing ability. It's also about the way she presents herself, the way she interacts with her audience and injects herself into everything she says and does. That's what attracts people to her. She says, "I'm really happy to be me, and I'd like to think people like me more because I'm happy with myself and not because I refuse to conform to anything."

Look at the way you communicate with people. How can you put more of yourself into your communications to create an authentic, engaging and relatable personal brand?

Sharing your "genius" or expertise is important, but to draw people in, you need to share all the elements that make you "you". Your blogs, videos and keynotes must give people an insight into you as a person—not just you as the expert. What are your unique characteristics? What makes you different? If you can harness and share these qualities, you will be well on the way to creating a powerful and trusted personal brand.

Trust and truth

A question people often ask me is: How can I know if I can trust someone? We've all made the mistake of trusting the wrong person or not knowing if someone is authentic or trustworthy. I believe it's part art, part science. And yes, you can learn, although it might be the hard way.

One aspect of my personal branding work has been my ability to use my intuition when I think someone isn't telling me the full truth or something isn't adding up. I have to think like a search engine: how would their name come up in a search result? Once I had a client who was well qualified yet unable to get a job. After thinking about the reasons why his job search was unsuccessful, I decided to Google his email address. I discovered he had a profile on a website called LiarsCheatsandBastards.com. Now, it's not my job to judge, just to present the information, and there are two sides to every story.

The thing is, though, that people (i.e. clients and potential employers) won't tell you if they find out information like this. They simply won't go through the next step with you, whether it's buying something from you or taking you to the next stage in the recruitment process. It's up to you to manage your reputation. Google yourself and your email address regularly to ensure nothing is working against you.

After my divorce, I started to worry about some of the people I was dating. At one point, I dated what seemed to be a compulsive liar. He was slippery, and I couldn't put my finger on a few things. I had also just started my business and lacked time to pay too much attention until I realised something was seriously wrong. So, I decided to hire a private detective and, sure enough, I found out he'd been living a double life. He had been married for 10 years and had a son. After that, I decided I was going to get better at working people out. I undertook a course by Paul Ekman, a leading expert in emotional psychology and author of **Emotions Revealed,** to learn how to improve my skills in reading micro-expressions.

The course was life-changing. It has helped me enormously in being more careful about whom I work with. And I now have an amazing partner, Mark, so thankfully I don't have to use what I learned while going on dates anymore!

Most of us have been through an experience that has made us lose trust in someone and, as a result, we've become warier. It's the same for the members of our tribe. They also have had bad experiences and are cautious. They also have access to a wealth of information online, so to build trust, leaders must be more real, authentic and genuine than ever before.

So, what helps us become more authentic?

This question reminds me of an incredible woman I met in 2018. She had a skin condition called vitiligo, which causes the loss of skin colour in blotches as pigment-producing cells die or cease functioning. Vitiligo is a genetic condition and often the result of stress. It turns out this woman began experiencing vitiligo as she went through her divorce. She said that when she went to her local shopping centre, kids would moo at her. It made her feel terrible, so she used make-up to hide her condition.

A few years after her divorce, she decided to start dating again and met a great guy called Phil. He had no idea she had this skin condition until one day he paid her a surprise visit to give her some flowers. When she opened the door, she said she didn't know who got the bigger fright, him or her!

When they calmed down, Phil asked her what was on her face. She explained her condition, to which he replied, "I love you inside and out. I still think you're the most beautiful woman in the world. Have you considered there might be other people like you out there with the same condition, going through the same experiences as you?"

She hadn't. Together, they did some research and launched an Instagram account, which attracted a tribe of people with the same condition. They created a hashtag called #theskinimin so people could share stories about their condition. Today, she speaks in schools, universities and conferences about how to be your most authentic self.

She also no longer wears make-up, is a model and has a loyal following. She continues to inspire people to love and accept themselves the way they are.

The key to this inspirational woman's success and renewed confidence was her tribe. When you build a tribe through your authenticity, you don't need the approval and validation of people who don't matter. Being in business for yourself can be isolating and lonely, so having a tribe that supports you and that you support in turn is critical.

Anthropologist and expert on tribes, Robin Dunbar, identified that successful tribes and groups operate in groups of 5, 15 and 150, with a greater village going to 1500. According to Thought Leaders Global founder and author of 10 books on Leadership, Matt Church, in today's world, we have another layer, with our "villages" reaching 15,000 thanks to social media.

For leaders and business owners going through extreme growth, it's easy to focus too much on the 1500 and 15,000 and lose sight of their closest tribe members. Think of your closest tribe members as your board of directors. They have the greatest influence over your success. Without them, you're pulled in every direction, spread thin. You lose your identity, and popularity; vanity metrics, search engines and hashtags drive you. You become what your 15,000 want you to be rather than your authentic self.

TRIBES

YOU
15 FAMILY
150 FRIENDS
1,500 FANS
15,000 FOLLOWERS

© Jane Anderson

If you've lost sight of your authentic self, it's time to bring in your 15. Who has trodden the path you want to tread? Who is in your corner? Who directly impacts your growth? Who are you trying to become?

Stop feeling alone and start feeling strong. Do the work your board advises you to do.

Eagles don't flock; you need to find them and build your tribe.

Being your most authentic self means creating an environment and tribe where you feel loved and accepted for whom you are. The more time you spend with those who value you, the more you can see you don't need to be someone else. You can be you, and you will build a higher level of trust. People will feel safe around you because they know whom they're dealing with.

When you feel you belong, you help others in your tribe feel like they belong, too. They have the confidence to be themselves. In the words of Brene Brown, "True belonging doesn't require you to change who you are. It requires you to be who you are."

QUESTIONS

1. Who are the 15 people who have the most significant influence on your success?

2. Where do you feel most alive and at your best?

3. Which friends and family value what you have to say the most?

4. Who makes you feel like you can be yourself?

5. Who are your 150?

6. Do you waste time, energy and effort on people who are not in your 15 or 150?

7. If so, what can you do to reduce the amount of time you spend with them without feeling guilty?

NOTES

[1] https://www.youtube.com/watch?v=qB5y9rRc1qs&feature=youtu.be

Credibility |

CHAPTER SIX

"Credibility is a leader's currency. With
it, he or she is solvent; without it, he or
she is bankrupt."

– *John Maxwell*

Helen Keller was born in 1880 in Tuscumbia, Alabama. She was the first of two
daughters born to Arthur H. Keller and Katherine Adams Keller and had two
older stepbrothers. Keller's father had served as an officer in the Confederate
Army during the Civil War, but the family was not wealthy. They earned an
income from their cotton plantation and later, Arthur became the editor of the
North Alabamian, a weekly local newspaper.

Keller was born with her senses of sight and hearing. She started speaking
when she was six months old and began walking at one year of age. However,
in 1882, when she was 19 months old, Keller contracted an illness that caused
a high body temperature. Her doctor described it as "brain fever", but experts
now believe it might have been scarlet fever or meningitis. Within a few days,

Keller's mother noticed she no longer reacted to the dinner bell or a hand waved in front of her face. She had lost her sight and hearing.

Keller was taken to see inventor Alexander Graham Bell, who, at the time, was working with deaf children. Bell suggested she visit the Perkins Institute for the Blind in Boston, where one of the school's most recent graduates, Anne Sullivan, was hired to work with her. Sullivan taught Keller, who could not see, hear or speak clearly, to communicate with the world around her. Their strong bond lasted for 49 years.

Incredibly, Keller went on to become a respected author, lecturer and world-renowned activist for people with disabilities. She received many honours in recognition of her accomplishments, including the Theodore Roosevelt Distinguished Service Medal in 1936, the Presidential Medal of Freedom in 1964, and election to the Women's Hall of Fame in 1965. She also received honorary doctoral degrees from Temple University and Harvard University, and the universities of Glasgow, Scotland; Berlin, Germany; Delhi, India; and Witwatersrand in Johannesburg, South Africa. Additionally, she was named an Honorary Fellow of the Educational Institute of Scotland.

Keller died in 1968, just a few weeks before her 88th birthday. Her ability to overcome her extraordinarily difficult circumstances makes Keller a powerful example of how determination, hard work and imagination can allow a person to triumph over adversity.[1]

Keller achieved incredible credibility against all the odds. Her remarkable accomplishments and the way she managed herself are a testament to that. She embodies the essence of a credible and trusted leader.

When you have credibility, not only do others trust you, but you also feel more in control because you can trust yourself. You gain a sense of personal responsibility. You know you can achieve results no matter what challenges you face. Essentially, credibility is your personal power.

If you don't work on your credibility, it's like you're stuck in a pinball machine, pushed around by circumstances. You feel like an imposter, as though you'll fall over with the slightest knock and people find out who you "really" are. Step outside the pinball machine and take control of your credibility. Guide it to where you want it to go.

———————————

"For a man to conquer himself is the first and noblest of all victories."
- Plato

———————————

The importance of self-awareness

Gary Vaynerchuk, best-selling author and key influencer around marketing and business growth, says self-awareness is the most powerful tool you can have in your leader's toolkit.

Furthermore, Dee Hock, founder and former CEO of Visa, says, "We should invest 50 per cent of our leadership amperage in self-leadership and the remaining 50 per cent should be divided into leading down, up and laterally."

Self-leadership is critical to your credibility as a leader. It's about self-management and personal responsibility. Think of it as driving a manual car as opposed to being in a self-driving Tesla car. You need to focus on your purpose and where you want to go rather than letting it drive for you. You need to have a plan, a high sense of focus, discipline, control of your circumstances and conviction. You need to take control of the day. Otherwise, the day will control you.

So, why do some people get ahead but others don't? Why do some stand out? Why do some people seem to say the right things but can't do the job?

I grew up in Lismore in northern New South Wales. Part of growing up there is knowing you can expect a flood. The town gets flooded about every seven years. Each year, emergency services announce on the radio what level the river is expected to rise to, so business owners can prepare. Recently, a levee bank was completed to stop water coming into the town when it rained. However, a once-in-100-years flood rushed through the town after an incredible downpour in a short period. There was no radio warning, so many business owners did nothing and lost much of their stock.

Those who'd had their businesses in town for many years knew not to leave anything to chance and had moved their stock and fittings to higher ground. In other words, the businesses owners who had a high level of self-leadership didn't wait to find out if their businesses were going to get flooded. They were proactive and took matters into their own hands. A failure to anticipate danger and act is not a sign of self-leadership.

Self-leadership is key to your credibility and success as a trusted leader. Green Peak Partners conducted a study of 72 executives in public and private companies with a turnover of $50 million to $5 billion.[2] It identified that a high self-awareness score was the strongest predictor of the overall success of the company. The executives also had a greater likelihood of being able to hire someone who was better on task and could make better decisions about things that weren't within the executive's skill set.

Daniel Goleman, the author of *Emotional Intelligence,* says exceptional leaders distinguish themselves through their superior self-leadership. But what are the elements of self-leadership? Researcher Dr John Ng divides self-leadership into four areas:[3]

1. Self-awareness. Acknowledging your values, strengths, weaknesses and emotional needs.

2. Self-management. The ability to nurture and harness your passions, abilities, emotions and decisions.

3. Other-awareness. Recognising the passions, strengths, weaknesses, potential and needs of others.

4. Other-management. The ability to grow and motivate people to reach their potential and fulfil the organisation's objectives.

While these are four powerful areas of self-leadership, I find it useful to drill even deeper. Keep the following, more specific areas front of mind as you strive to improve your credibility as a leader and influencer:

• Stress management

How do you face adversity, challenges and issues? How long does it take you to overcome those challenges and what strategies do you use? Do you take your stress out on others? How do you identify stress early and proactively manage it?

• Decision-making

How quickly do you make decisions? Do you know when to go ahead or delay? Do you procrastinate? How do you identify the issues involved in a complex problem? Do you take all parties into account? How aware are you of your environment so you can anticipate issues? How do you reduce decision fatigue?

• Consistency

An important factor in building trust is predictability. For example, to date, Tesla is trying to create a self-driving vehicle that is 100% safe. To ensure this, it needs to be 10 times more reliable than a human driver. It must be capable of making swift judgement calls and stop when a pram, kangaroo or truck comes in its direction. This not only requires an incredible amount of testing and data, it means humans must come to terms with relinquishing their control and trusting the car completely. At the moment, only 21% of Australians say they would trust a driverless car.[4] Self-driving cars have a long way to go to achieve credibility. It will take time and a proven track record. It's the same for leaders— the more predictable and consistent your actions and results are, the more credibility and trust you will build.

• Time management

Of all the aspects of self-leadership, I believe time management has the greatest impact on credibility. When you manage your time effectively and efficiently, your ability to achieve results stands out far more than someone who is just a smooth talker.

Did you know that more than 50% of people work at least an extra 10 hours per on top of their standard 38 hour week? That's almost 50 hours per week.[5] Meanwhile, many start-up entrepreneurs work about 80 hours per week.[6]

I often work with people who are burnt out, exhausted and disempowered in their work. They've tried to do too much, they've tried to do more with less, and they've tried unsuccessfully to manage the overwhelm of complex decisions and tasks on a day-to-day basis. In the words of productivity consultant David Allen, "You can do anything, but not everything."

I find that most people's calendars are full of meetings and nothing else. There's no time allocated for their own work or administrative tasks, such as processing emails, making phone calls and all the little things that must get done. This is a recipe for personal and professional disaster.

You need to manage your time more than it manages you. This means having an empowered calendar. An empowered calendar ensures you spend your time making progress. It helps you focus on traction instead of friction. It will create a high return on the investment of your time and advance your career and business much more rapidly.

There are five key things you can do to manage your time and personal productivity, empower your calendar and increase your credibility:

1. Allocate time for your work

If your day is full of meetings, you probably won't get started on your work until 5pm when everybody else has gone home. This is a sure-fire way to exhaustion. You need to make yourself and your work the number-one priority in your calendar. Only after you prioritise your work should you allocate meetings and other people's needs.

It's also essential you allocate time for your big projects and goals. In his book, **The 7 Habits of Highly Effective People**, Stephen Covey says you've got to have the "big rocks" in your calendar first. If you don't schedule the big items and instead only include all the "small rocks", you'll be unable to fit the more important things in later. The smaller rocks will consume all that space.

It's also helpful to break your projects down into smaller, manageable tasks. Estimate how long each task will take and put those times into your calendar. Most people tend to put these smaller tasks on a to-do list. The problem is if the job is going to take more than 10 minutes, they usually don't get done and the project stalls. So, it's important you calendarize them.

2. Batch communications

It's easy to lose time to frequent interruptions. Research tells us that when you are interrupted, it takes about 25 minutes to go back to what you were doing.[7] We tend to blame others for interrupting us, but these people aren't mind readers. They don't know what you're working on or that you're concentrating. They typically want to tell you about an idea, the latest development or their weekend. Sometimes, they want to vent.

If you allow these interruptions to continue, you will become a garbage dump. Everybody will dump their stuff on you. It's up to you to create boundaries around your time. An efficient way of dealing with interruptions is to batch communications with people who regularly interrupt you. Rather than letting them interrupt you five times a day, create a list of these people and connect with them during mutually agreed times.

Now, I'm not saying you can't interrupt each other if it's an urgent situation. But if it can wait, leave it for that pre-allocated time in your calendar. This way, the person is reassured they'll be able to speak with you. This one simple act can save you almost 1.5-2 hours per day.

3. Recovery time

Stephen Covey found that even high-performing organisations and individuals spend 25% of their time on urgent, important yet unexpected tasks. The problem is that most people don't expect the unexpected and get frustrated when the unforeseen does arise.

Although we spend about a quarter of our time on things we didn't anticipate, our calendars generally don't reflect this. What you need to do is allocate time in your calendar for "recovery". By recovery, I mean catch up on tasks and deal with the unexpected. If you have been away travelling, in a workshop or on leave, you will need some recovery time to process emails and deal with urgent enquiries once you're back online. If you can allocate about 25% of your day to important tasks you didn't expect, it will relieve stress and help you feel more empowered in your day.

4. Batch process anything that will take 10 minutes or less

If you look at your to-do list, all the tasks listed will have different completion times. Too often, we spend inordinate amounts of time working on little jobs. It's impossible to feel empowered and work on our credibility as leaders when we lose so much time this way.

To become more efficient, you need to allocate time in your calendar for batch processing tasks that will take 10 minutes or less. These tasks could include calling the bank, filing or sending an email. By batching these smaller tasks, you reduce the amount of friction in your day. You aren't constantly switching between different headspaces and creating decision fatigue. You'll also stay far more focussed when working on your bigger projects and tasks.

5. Break projects down into smaller, more manageable tasks

Humans aren't wired for longer, larger projects. We're built for the small, here and now. We get a rush of endorphins when we tick things off our to-do list, so there is a high incentive to get the little things done.

However, in a world where organisations need more project-based workers, we need to think bigger than in the past. The challenge is that the average person isn't shown how to do this. The key to implementation is to break the project into manageable tasks, then allocate time in your calendar for each activity. Without this step, delays ensue, the project loses priority, timeframes and budgets blow out. The truth is, we underestimate what we can do in a lifetime but overestimate what we can do in a day. The secret is progress, not perfection, through small, incremental steps.

If you can do these five things, you'll have a calendar that works for you. You'll feel more empowered in your leadership, knowing your time isn't lost. You'll feel more fulfilled in your work, have a greater sense of achievement and be able to focus on building your credibility and trust as a leader. You will be in control of your day. With an empowered calendar, you will make progress and achieve your potential.

Industry leadership

Tracey Hughes was born in the UK and backpacked to Australia in her teens. At 18 years of age, she took up a hairdressing apprenticeship. After proving to be a good stylist, Tracey was asked to attend an event to show people how she cut. Not really understanding what this meant, she agreed and was relieved she didn't have to speak; all she had to do was show people what she did.

What she didn't know was that she would have to commentate and explain the way she was cutting. On stage, she froze. Then she took a deep breath and somehow was able to explain what she was doing. It seemed she had an unrealised ability to speak in public. Before she knew it, she was asked to speak to even more audiences who wanted to learn about her unique style of cutting.

Today, Tracey graces the global stage. She's spoken to more than 500,000 salon professionals and has more than 20,000 Instagram followers. She also has a bevy of awards to her name. These include:

• Certified Speaking Professional

• International Haircut of the Year

• 4 x Educator of the Year

- 4 x Excellence in Education
- 10 x Salon of the Year
- 2 x Hairdresser of the Year
- 2 x Creative Colourist of the Year
- Australian Masters
- People's Choice

One thing that sets Tracey apart is her value proposition. She is 100% committed to the customer experience, whether she's presenting to audiences from the stage or working with customers in her salon. This has been Tracey's "front wheel" for her entire working career.

In **The Discipline of Market Leaders,** authors Michael Treacy and Fred Wiersema detailed their research into 80 market-leading industries. They identified three key drivers or wheels that an industry-leading organisation should have. These are:

- *Operational excellence*
- *Product leadership*
- *Customer intimacy*

Treacy and Wiersema claim that as an industry leader, you need to choose one of these as your front wheel. If you try to do all three, you'll be spread too thin and fail to be "known for knowing something".

In an expert's world, this approach works on two levels: knowing what your customer's front wheel is so you can speak the same language, and understanding what your front wheel is so you play to your strengths.

Industry leadership is crucial to removing commoditisation. There is no point having your name and a big price on your services if you can't prove you're the best at what you do. Customers will pay for the level of an industry leader, provided you can give evidence you are the best. It's like offering the choice between first class, business class or economy. As an industry leader, we're more likely first and business class. We lead the way for economy. You are the trendsetter!

You need to undertake certain activities to demonstrate you are an industry leader. Some of these activities include:

• Speaking at industry events and conferences, possibly even globally.

• Undertaking PR activities, such as media interviews and writing for publications.

• Winning and/or being nominated for industry awards.

• Setting prices that represent industry leadership standard.

• Being on industry committees and groups.

• Mentoring others in the industry.

These are just a few ways you can not only stand out in a noisy world, but also shape an industry, have an impact on a larger and deeper scale, and deepen your message and identity as a credible, trusted leader.

QUESTIONS

1. What do you think gives you credibility in your organisation, business or tribe?

2. How do you know?

3. How consistent are you in your decision-making?

4. How do your emotions affect your decision-making?

5. How do your emotions affect your decision-making under pressure?

6. How well do you recognise the strengths of others?

7. On a scale of 1-10, how well do you think you manage your time?

NOTES

[1] "Helen Keller Biography," Biography, April 2, 2014. https://www.biography.com/people/helen-keller-9361967

[2] "New Study Shows Nice Guys Finish First," American Management Association. https://www.amanet.org/training/articles/new-study-shows-nice-guys-finish-first.aspx?pcode=XCRP

[3] "Creative Self-Leadership," Creativity Squads. http://creativitysquads.com/creative-self-leadership/

[4] Adam Luehrs, "Seven Problems Self-Driving Cars Need to Overcome," Smith's Lawyers, August 13, 2018. https://www.smithslawyers.com.au/post/self-driving-car-problems

[5] Maurie Backman, "Here's How Many Hours the Average American Works Per Year," The Motley Fool, December 17, 2017. https://www.fool.com/careers/2017/12/17/heres-how-many-hours-the-average-american-works-pe.aspx

[6] Kathleen Elkins, "Self-made millionaires agree on how many hours you should be working to succeed," Make It, June 15, 2017. https://www.cnbc.com/2017/06/15/self-made-millionaires-agree-on-how-many-hours-you-should-be-working.html

[7] Blake Thorne, "How Distractions At Work Take Up More Time Than You Think," I Done This, July 23, 2015. http://blog.idonethis.com/distractions-at-work/

CHAPTER SEVEN

Advocacy |

"Unless someone like you cares a
whole awful lot, nothing is going to
get better. It's not."

– Dr Seuss

A few years ago, I worked for a large organisation with about 10,000 staff. I had a great team of five who worked hard, were incredibly loyal and passionate about their jobs. As the team leader, my role was to ensure the delivery of 25 significant projects throughout the year. Most of my team had come from the frontline, so they had a high level of expertise.

I trusted them with how they managed their time and got their work done. Many members of my team would come in early and work late, and we rallied together when the pressure was on. It was such a great team. Me being the trusting person I am, I gave them complete autonomy. I said that as long as they could get the work done, I wouldn't clock watch. They were responsible for their results. In this way, we changed the previous team's reputation of being difficult to work with to being collaborative, forming strong relationships and achieving great results.

About a year into my job, a new member joined the HR senior team. Sarah (not her real name) was relatively new in her role as the Head of People Engagement. I was the Head of Learning and Development. Sarah didn't have any staff reporting to her and seemed to have a real issue with my team, which was the largest team in the department.

We were in a meeting with our boss one day when Sarah decided to attack my team, saying they were lazy and all I did was "see them playing ping pong in the tea room". Things had been rumbling for a while, but I didn't expect this.

My boss didn't say anything, just looked at the floor. So, I leant across the table and said, "You've been here all of five minutes. You walk in at 9am on the dot and leave at 4pm on the dot. You have no idea that my team has been in the office since 7am, delivering on deadlines. In fact, how I run my team is none of your business, but if you really want to know, we have 24 major projects to roll out—that's six each quarter. It's about time you started to put a bit more focus on your deliverables and not on what everyone else is doing or not doing. It's starting to look like you don't actually know how to do your job. So, I suggest you start doing some of the work you're being paid to do, stop criticising everyone and start getting something done."

Then, I left the meeting.

I realised a few things. My boss didn't stand up for me. I was disappointed that I had to fight my own battle and she didn't back me. I knew we were making massive inroads with stakeholders and it had taken a year to get there. My boss knew this but said nothing.

Word got around about the meeting and a few of my team members asked me about it. What they said will stay with me for a long time. They said, "Thanks so much for standing up for us."

I hadn't thought about the impact of that until then, but of course, I had just been on the receiving end of someone I trusted not stand up for me.

From that day, I noticed my team and I connected even more. It was like a deeper camaraderie had been created because our credibility was challenged for the first time. We talked more about how we stood up for each other and had each other's back. The conversation and discussion it created was immensely valuable and taught me how powerful advocacy is for a leader to build trust.

In 2017, nurses were ranked the most trusted profession in the US, according to the annual Gallup poll on honesty and ethical standards. In fact, nurses have topped the list of 22 professions for 16 years. Most Americans polled (82 per cent) described nurses' ethics as high or very high. The least trusted professions were real estate agents, advertisers and car salesmen.[1]

Why are nurses the most trusted profession? They help people when they're at their most vulnerable. They are their voice, often in critical situations. They act in the patients' best interests and translate what is happening to them in a way that's easy to understand.

As a trusted leader, you, too, must be a voice for your people. You must advocate for them and keep their best interests at heart.

Critical to this is your ability to educate them.

The power of education

Technology is changing the way people learn. This is probably most evident when you look at the way people now self-diagnose their health problems. Having access to "Doctor Google" means people are doing their own research into their symptoms. They are more likely to challenge their doctors' diagnoses and seek a second opinion. Medical professionals must work harder to build trust with their patients.

Savvy medical practitioners know that to have greater trust and influence with their patients, they need to educate them. A great example of a medical professional with a position of high trust is Dr Grant Duong, also known as "the Foot Mechanic". Dr Duong is a podiatrist based in Sydney. He has a strong following on Instagram, where he educates people about foot health in an informative and entertaining way.

Education plays a significant role in nurturing people's trust in you. When you can show people you understand their problems and challenges, they can see you can help them and are more likely to follow you. And one of the most effective ways of educating people and advocating for them is writing blog posts.

"Education is the most powerful weapon which you can use to change the world."

– Nelson Mandela

Blogging

In August 2011, I received a call from a new client who wanted to meet with me to discuss a program they were looking at running in their organisation. I hadn't met this person before, so I made sure I prepared for the meeting.

In the past, I had spent a lot of time during my sales meetings establishing my credibility, identifying the unique angle or expertise I could bring and what the program would involve. In this particular instance, the task was to make more than 200 people redundant in an outplacement program. The client would then usually go away, have a think about it and regroup.

This day was different. When I arrived at the meeting, the client had already decided they wanted to work with me. In fact, all they wanted to do was decide on dates for their program.

I was surprised and wondered how this had happened, especially since I didn't know them. What had happened was the client had found my blog. By that stage, I had written more than 40 articles on the topic, and they had read most of them. They were already confident I could deliver what they needed. That one meeting secured six months of delivery and changed the career direction of more than 200 people, who either started their own businesses or commenced new jobs by the end of the program.

Blogging is a cost-effective, efficient way to educate people. It engages them with your brand and is essential for establishing your thought leadership.

Think of it as letting your potential clients take you for a test drive. We've all come across the stereotypical car dealer who can only think of getting their commission. But before we buy, we need to get to know the car. We can't be hurried into a decision. We need to know if it's safe and economical. We need to know if it feels right. How do we do this? We take it for a spin.

Take your audience on a test drive into your world. Show them your insights and perspective through your blog. Give them a solid understanding of who you are and what you do. When written effectively, blog posts also act as a mirror: the reader sees themselves and their issues in what you're saying.

As an influencer, you can't afford not to blog. Research shows that marketers who blog receive 67% more leads than those who do not.[2] Furthermore, 81% of US online consumers trust information and advice from blogs and 61% have made a purchase based on recommendations from a blog.[3]

Regular blog posts are also a fantastic way of boosting your search engine optimisation (SEO). The more relevant content you have on your website, the more likely you will turn up in online search results. By using your targeted keywords in your blog posts and publishing consistently, you'll have a more viable online presence.

Write valuable content

To generate leads, drive customer action and build trust, your blog posts must add value. Your audience must walk away feeling as though they have learned something or gained a valuable insight. But sometimes, we are so close to our topic that we fail to look objectively at what we write.

How do you know if your content adds value? According to **Forbes**, your content is valuable "if people seek it out, if people want to consume it, rather than avoiding it."4 The idea is to get people to come back for more. You want to create blog posts that people share and comment on.

To ensure your blog posts are engaging, educational and valuable, you need to:

1. Be clear about your message and your audience. It's surprising how many blogs have so much to say yet fail to deliver a punchline. What's the point of what you're saying? What's your takeaway message? Who is your target audience and what do you want them to walk away with? How would you like them to act on the information you're giving them? Your message and your audience will also help you determine your tone of voice. Will your message have more impact if it's written in a conversational style? Or should it have a more instructional tone?

2. Make it unique. Don't regurgitate the same message everyone else is making. Offer something new. What do you have to say that no one else is saying? What makes you different? How can you get your message across by sharing your unique stories and perspective?

3. Use images. Enhance your content with photos, illustrations and infographics. The strategic use of images will not only break up the text and make your posts visually appealing; they can also help you emphasise a point and guide your readers through your ideas.

4. Have a clear structure. You're not writing a book, but blog posts still need structure. Without clearly organising your content, your message will get confused, and your audience will stop reading. Use subheadings, bullet points and regular paragraph breaks to help with the flow of content.

5. Use links. Hyperlink words or sentences that relate to other pages on your website. This not only boosts your SEO, but it also encourages readers to linger on your website for longer and consume more content.

And remember to proofread your blog posts. Poor spelling and grammar detract from your message and undermine your positioning as a respected industry leader. A good rule of thumb is to write your post, edit it, then wait 24 hours before you give it a final proofread. This gives you the clear headspace you need to detect errors that otherwise might have gone undetected in a rush to get it published.

Create a call to action

A call to action is the icing on the blog post cake. It's a clickable link, button or image that prompts your readers to act. If you've given your readers informative, compelling content, by the time they reach the end of your post, they should feel inspired and motivated. Don't let them read and run. Ask them to act on their motivation.

Be clear and specific about your call to action. What would you like your audience to do? What is your objective? For example, if you want to build your client database, provide a button that links to your e-newsletter opt-in form. If you have a book you want to sell, direct your audience to your shop. If you want readers to sign up to a workshop, create a button that links to your registration page.

Make your call to action as simple and clear as possible. Your readers will see it as the next logical step and be more likely to click that button.

Sensemaking: the new way of marketing to build trust

"A strong woman stands up for herself. A stronger woman stands up for everyone else."
- Unknown

In 1999, when I was 18, my family and I spent the summer in Europe. It was our version of the Griswold's European Vacation. My dad was the driver and I was the navigator. My job was to read the map and ensure we didn't take a wrong turn. Back then, we didn't have Google Maps or mobile phones, but fortunately, we only made one wrong turn.

The countries we travelled through included Austria, Switzerland, Italy, France, Germany and Holland. When we went to France, we had to find accommodation as we hadn't booked any in advance. None of my family spoke French, but I had spent five years studying French in high school. It was my main subject in Year 12.

So, it was up to me to find accommodation in France. I had to go through the travel books, decide where we should go, make some phone calls and have conversations in French to find somewhere for us to say. I found a place that sounded perfect, so I called them. The gentleman on the other end of the line greeted me with, "Bonjour?" *(Hello?)*

I replied, "Bonjour, oui. Vous avez un nuit pour cinque personnes s'il vous plait" *(Hello, yes. Do you have a room for five people for tonight please?)*

"Oui. Ca fait 120 francs" *(That will be 120 francs.)*

"Tres bien, merci. Nous sommes arrivee a 5pm." *(Great, thank you. We'll arrive at 5pm.)*

We managed to secure a room for the night, and the rest of the trip went beautifully.

Essentially, I held a position of trust in my family. If I hadn't been able to speak French, I wouldn't have been able to talk to the locals. I wouldn't have been able to translate for my family and finding accommodation would have taken a lot longer. We could have ended up somewhere unsafe or out of the way. We would have lost time feeling stressed instead of having a great holiday.

It's the same for an influencer. Your job is that of a translator. There is so much information available on the internet; you need to translate it for your tribe. Ensure your content is relevant, concise and valuable. In other words, you are sensemaking—making sense of all the information available on your area of expertise. The benefit of this is that you save people time. They trust you because you've consistently shared knowledge that's useful, relevant and remarkable.

I often find when I'm working with experts, influencers and personally branded businesses that they hold back from sharing their knowledge. They fear no one will follow them or read what they have to say. They think that because people can already get the information elsewhere, what's the point?

The key is to tailor your content to a targeted audience. In an interview with business growth expert Kerwin Rae, futurist and strategic planning consultant Dr Keith Suter says there is a global shift in the media from broadcasting information to "narrowcasting" information. Broadcasting information means sending one standard piece of content to a broad audience. Narrowcasting, on the other hand, means sending tailored content to a narrow, specific group of people.[5] You are more likely to make more of an impact on the right kind of people this way. You don't need millions of followers.

Perhaps you are a micro-influencer and have a level of trust with a small group of people. This is when sensemaking comes to the fore. Sensemaking means making sense of or giving meaning to experiences and new developments.

A sensemaker is like a translator. They translate what is happening into something meaningful and relevant for their tribe.

To start translating for your audience, firstly, you must get clarity on your area of expertise. Secondly, identify what it is you can educate people about, regardless of whether information on the topic already exists. And thirdly, ignore what everybody else is saying—stay focussed on what you know. Explain to others what it means for them in their world, align it with the challenges and problems they experience, and share with them your solutions.

If you do this, you will be far more focussed on serving the needs of your tribe. You will become a true advocate for them, working in their best interests rather than focusing only on yourself. You will shift from attention in to attention out.

QUESTIONS

1. Who in your team or organisation may feel too intimidated or shy to voice their opinions?

2. What are their greatest challenges or fears?

3. What activities can you undertake to ensure they have their needs or concerns addressed?

4. What do you think holds them back?

5. If you ask them, what do they say holds them back?

6. Which clients or customers follow you online but are too afraid to connect?

7. How often do you reach out to them?

NOTES

[1] Megan Brenan, "Nurses Keep Healthy Lead as Most Honest, Ethical Profession," Gallup, December 26, 2017. https://news.gallup.com/poll/224639/nurses-keep-healthy-lead-honest-ethical-profession.aspx

[2] Olivia Allen, "6 Stats You Should Know About Business Blogging in 2015," HubSpot, March 11, 2015. https://blog.hubspot.com/marketing/business-blogging-in-2015

[3] Jeff Charles, "10 Important Reasons Entrepreneurs Need to Take Blogging Seriously," Huffington Post, December 6, 2017. https://www.huffingtonpost.com/jeff-charles/10-important-reasons-entr_b_10964854.html

[4] Josh Steimle, "What Is Content Marketing?", Forbes, September 19, 2014. https://www.forbes.com/sites/joshsteimle/2014/09/19/what-is-content-marketing/#3410333410b9

[5] "Dr. Keith Suter – Is the World Really Doomed?" Kerwin Rae. https://www.kerwinrae.com/dr-keith-suter

CHAPTER EIGHT

Empathy |

"The great gift of human beings
is that we have the power of
empathy."

– Meryl Streep

At the very core of building trust is empathy, and that is why it is in the middle of the Trusted Leader model.

Without empathy, there can be no insight or understanding, only ego and assumptions. Often, we can be so preoccupied with appearing as though we have the right solutions, we jump straight into solving problems for people rather than taking them on a journey. It's essential we give them the opportunity to not only to trust us but also to articulate the emotions, challenges and fears they are experiencing.

9 PILLARS OF THE TRUSTED LEADER

———————— T R U S T ————————

ME	YOU	WE
3 Productivity	**6** Connection	**9** Truth
CREDIBILITY	**VULNERABILITY**	**TRANSPARENCY**
Control	Shame	Fear
2 Genuine	**5** Understanding	**8** Respect
AUTHENTICITY	**EMPATHY**	**EQUALITY**
Manipulation	Assumptions	Status
1 Clarity	**4** Voice	**7** Safety
IDENTITY	**ADVOCACY**	**HUMILITY**
Validation	Self-serving	Ego

CONNECTION

© Jane Anderson

I believe driving change is a bit like landing a plane. You must clear the tarmac first before it's safe to land. Leaders often feel frustrated because they can't get their message through. They've lacked empathy and failed to clear the tarmac and gain clearance from ground control to land their solution. I haven't always been perfect at this myself and have learned the hard way how to drive change effectively!

Empathy is "attention out". It's about diverting the focus from your own needs to the needs of others.

I'm a member of faculty of the Thought Leaders Business School, where we work with 150 of the world's leading experts in their field, helping them grow their practices to the $1 million-plus mark and beyond. One of our mantras is to be "attention out". I happened to win the inaugural award for this in 2018. Thought Leaders founder Matt Church describes attention out as "always being in service and generously giving advice, support and kindness to the tribe". The more attention you give with the intention of supporting and helping others, the more trust you will gain in any tribe.

When you're in a position of trust and influence, it's important to remember this position encompasses "Titular Power". Also known as formal power, Titular Power refers to the power that comes with having a specific title or role, usually from a place in a hierarchy.[1]

For example, in 2018, Prince Harry and Meghan Markle were in Australia to launch the Invictus Games in Sydney. As part of their royal tour, they visited a country town called Dubbo where school children greeted them. Prince Harry knelt to say hello to a little boy who had been waiting enthusiastically. The boy was so fascinated by the Prince's beard, he began stroking it and gave him a big hug. Prince Harry was delighted by the gesture and thought it was funny. The boy's teacher was surprised because the crowd had been strictly briefed beforehand that there was to be no touching of the royal couple. However, the little boy couldn't have been more hands on. He even gave Meghan a hug, which was a beautiful thing to see.

As leaders, it's easy to forget that others may perceive us as intimidating. But in the case of the royal couple, the boy wasn't intimidated at all. He truly wanted to connect with them.

Leaders, by default, hold a position of authority. The problem is that this power can disconnect you from the people you lead. You may have built an imaginary wall between you and your customers or you and your team members without even realising it. When this happens, people will be hesitant to connect with you because of fear—fear they're going to lose their job, fear they're not good enough, fear you won't care and fear that they might come across as silly or stupid.

It's important for leaders to shift from intimidation to intimacy—without losing credibility. When you remove intimidation, you increase connection.

You show empathy for your people and can support them through change.

If you don't remove the intimidation factor, your level of influence suffers, and your ability to help people through change takes much longer. Change can still occur, but it will happen from a place of fear or coercion. People will feel frustrated and may stop following you. In other words, intimidation stunts and limits your growth. It prevents you from playing big and it makes you play small.

In his book, **Soft Power,** Joseph Nye explains that power is the ability to influence the behaviour of others to get the outcomes you want. You can change others' behaviour by threatening them, paying them or finding a cooperative way to get them on board to do what you want.

On the other hand, soft power is about creating engagement. It's the ability to obtain your preferred outcomes through attraction rather than coercion or payment.

Kobe Bryant, one of the greatest basketball players of all time, once said, "Intimidation doesn't exist if you're in the right frame of mind." And if you can get into the right frame of mind, you'll be able to focus more on a higher purpose and outcome, whether it be for an individual or organisation.

Recently, I saw author and award-winning copywriter Sean D'Souza speak at the We Are Podcast conference in Brisbane. In his book, **The Brain Audit: Why Customers Buy (And Why They Don't),** D'Souza delves into the psychology of buying behaviours. He stresses the importance of using empathy to unpack people's problems, fears and challenges. D'Souza says if you're a leader who fails to show empathy, your customers will feel so intimidated they will avoid dealing with you.

Several years ago, a client reached out to me after they'd seen me in one of my videos. They said, "Oh, you came across so authentic and real in video. I could hear your voice, so I decided to reach out because until then I thought maybe I wasn't good enough to work with you."

Often, leaders focus on the fact they are the authority. They assume they are the only source of truth, which is an arrogant mindset. When we fail to influence others positively, we come up against a wall. We need to break that wall so we can support people to achieve their goals.

Keeping this in mind, there are 10 ways you can reduce intimidation through empathy and build trust during times of change:

1. Active listening. This involves asking questions. Active listening allows you to meet people where they're at, reducing assumptions and unconscious biases. Prince Harry and Meghan Markle were highly present throughout their royal tour. They listened to the little boy when they were in Dubbo. They connected with him quickly. They knelt on the ground, maintained eye contact and were at his level. As leaders, we need to crouch a little more. We need to get to where people are, support them and lift them.

2. Ask for feedback. Thinking you know everything does not shift people's behaviour. One of the fastest ways you can grow your positioning as a trusted leader is to ask for others' opinions about what you could be doing differently. What's working well and what isn't? Ask them what they need from you so you can adapt and flex, based on their needs.

3. Be understanding. Share your feelings and encourage others to do the same. You don't necessarily have to agree with each other, but you need to try to understand from where the other person is coming. Only once you've found common ground can you find a way forward. It's even more important to keep this in mind if you have team members who come from different cultural backgrounds and have a different experience of power to you.

4. Build rapport. Rapport is not about manipulation. It's about creating a safe space and mutual trust. When you have a strong rapport with your team members and customers, they will feel comfortable enough to share their problems with you without feeling threatened.

5. Get to know people on a personal level. If you can learn more about people outside of the work they're doing, it humanises you and them. You will be able to gain more context about where your people are coming from and connect with them more easily. It will give you a greater insight into their world so you can adapt your approach and support them through change.

6. Set the environment for conversations. For example, sitting beside the person you're having a conversation with rather than opposite them helps strengthen your connection with them. For example, when I'm working with doctors who need to have difficult conversations with patients, I encourage them to sit beside the patient. They may even put their hand on their arm or use appropriate touch to comfort them. Sitting beside someone reduces physical intimidation. People will feel less threatened and be more open to sharing things with you.

7. Share stories. This is a powerful way to show empathy and reduce intimidation. Share stories about your successes but, more importantly, remember to share stories about your failures. People relate more to stories of struggle. Recently, I went to see a mentor of mine speak. During his presentation, he shared some experiences that didn't go well for him. I left his presentation feeling inspired and realised that while this person was amazing and seemed almost superhuman, he was still a person just like me. This realisation made me comfortable enough to say what I needed to say without feeling silly. It created a safe space between us because I knew my challenges had been his challenges, too. I could see he understood where I was coming from.

8. Think of leading as a service. It's important to have a service mindset when you're in a position of authority and power. Remember that while you may already have the title of leader, your behaviour needs to flip to the opposite, which is service. You're there to serve, support and identify what holds people back. The role of a leader is to guide people through change, and the only way you can do that is by having a mindset of supporting and serving others.

9. Be mindful of the groups you hang out with. People feel intimidated when they're on the outer. We all have a primal need to feel part of a tribe. As a leader, you need to ensure your people have a sense of belonging. If you only hang out with people who are in positions of power, it sends the message that others don't belong in your group. If you want to reduce intimidation and gain people's trust, you need to spend time with people in different circles.

10. Be visible. If you work in an organisation, remember to get out and lead by walking around. Have conversations with different people across all levels. If you're only seen in your office talking to the executive team or, equally, if you're an expert in your field and are only seen hanging out with the "cool" people, then people will struggle to relate to you and trust you. They won't feel worthy enough to talk to you. You need to be visible. So, get out there and talk to people. Demonstrate that you can connect with the average person. You'll be far more approachable, and people will feel they can talk to you. You'll also learn a lot more and be able to show empathy to lead people through change.

From leadership to humanship

"Leadership is about empathy. It is about having the ability
to relate to and connect with people for the purpose of inspiring
and empowering their lives."
- Oprah

One Friday afternoon, I was rushing down Elizabeth Street towards the Myer Centre car park in Brisbane City. I was late to get home to my partner Mark, who had dinner underway. Family was visiting, and I knew I was going to hit peak-hour traffic.

On my way, I hurried past one of the littlest old ladies I'd ever seen. She was like a fragile bird, slow and struggling with her bags. I noticed a sore on her leg. One of her bags kept hitting it; it must have been hurting her.

As I rushed past, I thought, "Hold on, what is she doing out on her own? Someone could steal her bag easily or knock her over if they don't see her."

So, I turned around to ask her where she was headed and offered to carry

118 • TRUSTED / JANE ANDERSON

her bag. She said she wanted to go to the food court for dinner but told me not to worry; she didn't want to be a bother. However, having a mother who had worked in aged care for 20 years, I knew she was far too frail to be on her own.

She seemed hesitant to let me help her, so I reassured her and said, "It's OK. I can understand you might not want me to carry your bags, but it's on my way."

We chatted all the way during the slow walk to the food court. I discovered she lived on her own and had spent Christmas Day in bed unwell, with no one visiting her. No meals on wheels, no family. Nothing. She said no one knew she lived on her own.

Over the past few years, she'd suffered a hit-and-run accident, which had crushed her arm. She said there was no follow-up when she was sent home from the hospital. She'd had her bag stolen three times and was in pain from the wound on her leg. Her rented apartment building had just been sold and she needed to move.

After much discussion over a Big Mac and fries, we exchanged contact details. I found out her name was Dot*. She then agreed for me to call the Department of Health and Ageing to check on her welfare.

I like to think people care enough to stop and check on people who are frail and alone. After hearing my mum's stories from working in aged care, I know you can never assume people aren't forgotten or haven't fallen through the cracks of the system.

I've also been fortunate enough to coach doctors and executives in the Department of Ageing, and I know how hard they work to ensure vulnerable people aren't overlooked. But the fact is, these things still happen. It takes nothing to check whether someone's OK, but I've learned that some people don't ask because they don't know what to say or do.

I wonder, how many of your customers or tribe members are like Dot? Do you assume they will ask for help if they need it? Often, they're struggling on their own and don't want to be a bother to anyone. But on the inside, they're frustrated, stressed and need your help.

Of course, we have systems and processes in place to help people. But systems don't have empathy, nor do they connect with us at a human level. As former Australian Defence Force chief David Hurley says, "The standard you walk past is the standard you accept."

What actions do you take to show empathy and understanding to others?

* Not her real name.

QUESTIONS

1. What are your tribe members' greatest challenges?

2. What are their fears?

3. How do you know?

4. What are your customers' greatest challenges and fears?

5. How do you know?

6. What assumptions have you made about others (clients, colleagues and stakeholders) that may not be true?

7. How can you challenge your biases and be open to identifying and understanding the issues of those who matter the most in your world?

NOTES

[1] Mark Murphy, "You Need To Know The 7 Types Of Power If You Want To Succeed," Forbes, March 19, 2017. https://www.forbes.com/sites/markmurphy/2017/03/19/you-need-to-know-the-7-types-of-power-if-you-want-to-succeed/#42bbe562536d

CHAPTER NINE

Vulnerability |

"I found that the more truthful and
vulnerable I was, the more empowering
it was for me."
– *Alanis Morrisette*

Most of us don't trust something if it seems too perfect. In the age of social media, the more real something seems, the more we tend to trust it. As leaders and entrepreneurs, when we attach our self-worth to what we are delivering, being "real" becomes even more of a challenge.

Recently, I worked with a government department and was introduced by one of the senior executive leaders before my presentation. During the introduction, she shared her journey of dealing with mental health challenges and depression.

I discovered that her experiences were well known amongst the staff. Everyone I spoke to said that as a result of her being so open about her struggles, they found her more real and relatable. They could connect her challenges with their own, and were inspired by the fact she was able to not only continue her work as a leader but as a female leader. Her openness meant they felt respected. They didn't feel embarrassed or ashamed to speak up about their challenges. A number of them said they felt more empowered knowing their well-being was valued at work.

Being vulnerable can be hard. It seems counterintuitive to reveal a side of yourself that may not appear strong when you want to be powerful, resilient and lead change. But when we are open about our vulnerability, we allow others to be vulnerable, too. We become more light, open and transparent, therefore creating greater trust with our tribe.

Most clients work with me because I share the challenges and fears I've had. They feel less judged, less ashamed and more accepted. I don't share my fears and challenges for validation; I share them because I've worked through those things and know how to help others avoid them, saving them time, energy, effort and sometimes a lot of tears and heartache. Therefore, my vulnerability helps them progress more, achieve more and do more.

When we are vulnerable, we create a deeper connection with others instead of having surface-level conversations. We're not as afraid of change or doing "the wrong thing". In fact, vulnerability breeds innovation. It gives us the space to try and test new ideas.

I deliver a business and leadership program called **Women with Influence,**[1] where we laugh at our failures each week. We call it "F'UP Friday". We not only laugh at ourselves, but we also share our learnings as part of our faults. In fact, my team uses this strategy. It permits us to have a conversation around the fact we're not perfect. We find out about mistakes in a safe way and can fix them without the person feeling incompetent or scared they'll get in trouble.

When you can be vulnerable, it's like you remove an invisible wall between you and your team or audience. The wall represents people's thoughts of not being good enough, not being smart enough. If you can remove the wall, you'll become far more connected as a team. There will be a much higher level of trust. And, as a result, you'll gain much more traction, motivation and transformation.

Brene Brown is a master of work around vulnerability and the author of the book, **Daring Greatly: How the Courage to be Vulnerable Transforms the Way We Live, Love, Parent, and Lead.** Brown's TED Talk, "The Power of Vulnerability", is one of the most viewed TED Talks of all time, with more than 37 million views.[2] In it, she reveals how she's learnt to embrace her vulnerability. She shares stories of people she's worked with and, based on her 12 years of research, covers her work on courage, worthiness and shame. She says, "We can't know things like love and belonging and joy and creativity without vulnerability."

Brown says what holds us back from being vulnerable is the armour of perfectionism. Perfectionism is, at its core, about trying to earn approval. She says most perfectionists grow up being praised for achievement and performance—through their grades at school, their manners, following the rules, pleasing people, the way they dressed. They believe they will get praised only if they get great results. The problem is that perfectionism correlates with depression, anxiety, addiction, paralysis and missed opportunities.

The fear of failure, the fear of making mistakes, the fear of not meeting people's expectations and being criticised leads us to a space of unhealthy competition. Perfectionism is not a way to avoid being vulnerable or feeling ashamed. Brown says perfectionism is a form of shame. When we struggle with perfectionism, we're struggling with shame. Vulnerability is neither victory nor defeat; it's both. It's about engaging and being all in.

As leaders, it pays to remember that when we lead people through times of change, they're experiencing fear. They're anxious, stressed and they feel as though things are out of their control. So, we have to be all in with them, and the only way we can be all in is by being vulnerable enough to share our fullest selves and show we are fully committed. By being vulnerable, we can have more profound and authentic connections with our people. We strengthen our credibility and have greater empathy for the experiences of our clients and teams.

It was author and spiritual activist **Marianne Williamson** who said: "Our deepest fear is not that we are inadequate. Our deepest fear is that we are powerful beyond measure. It is our light, not our darkness, that frightens us. We ask ourselves, "Who am I to be brilliant, gorgeous, and fabulous?" Actually, who are you not to be? You are a child of God. Your playing small does not serve the world. There is nothing enlightened about shrinking so that other people will not feel insecure around you. We are all meant to shine, as children do. We were born to manifest the glory of God that is within us. It is not just in some of us; it is in everyone, and as we let our own light shine, we unconsciously give others permission to do the same. As we are liberated from our own fear, our presence automatically liberates others."

So, what creates a safe environment for a leader to be vulnerable? It may seem like it's the chicken before the egg, that building trust creates vulnerability. But for leaders, I think they need to take the lead on this first. They need to be courageous enough to be vulnerable.

Vulnerability takes courage.
Courage takes overcoming fear.
Overcoming fear takes belief.
Gaining belief takes a sense of purpose.

I believe it takes three key elements for a leader to be comfortable with being vulnerable:

1. Courage

Mark Twain said, "Courage is resistance to fear, mastery of fear, not absence of fear". Courage is the ability to do something that frightens you. Being vulnerable as a leader seems counterintuitive. You may think, "What if people use it against me? Won't I lose respect?" Most leaders fear being wrong, failing or being "found out". And yes, these things may happen, but you will give more value to the those who follow you. Your journey will inspire them. You permit them to be their best selves, try new things and innovate. You give them the hope that they, too, can achieve greatness.

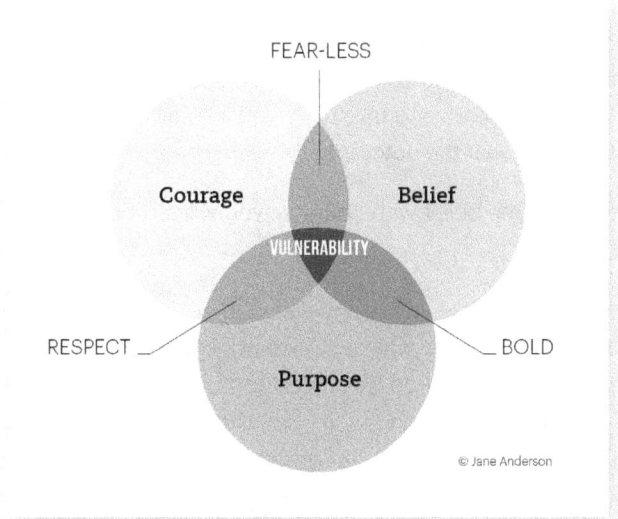

© Jane Anderson

Being courageous isn't necessarily about being the centre of attention. You don't need to sing from the rooftops, "Look at me, see how courageous I am." It's about putting one foot in front of the other and doing what matters. The more noise you make about it, the more pressure you create for yourself.

Recently, I was part of an event where I had to sing as part of a team. For those who don't know me, my greatest fear is singing, and I will avoid it at all costs! So, I decided to pretend singing was not my fear. I also chose not to tell anyone how scared I was. I knew if I did, I'd make the situation worse. So, I sang my part and hoped no one would notice. At the end of the performance, a member of the audience told me how great it was, and they felt "so lucky" because they couldn't believe they were seeing me rap on stage! This encouraged me not to be so afraid.

2. Belief

Belief is the acceptance or faith that something exists or is true, especially something that has no proof. Author Robert Collier once said, "Your chances of success in any undertaking can always be measured by your belief in yourself." When you haven't done something before, you lack evidence to prove it will work for you. If you're starting to work on your vulnerability, it can pay to have mentors and people around you whom you respect. They will provide a safe space for you as you learn and take risks. You will still be loved and accepted by them no matter what the outcome.

When you combine belief with courage, you will still have fear, but you will fear a little less.

Another way to increase your self-belief is to get out of your comfort zone regularly. The more you do what you already know how you do, the more you decrease your confidence. You need to push yourself and set goals to try things you have never done before. Be your own best friend during these times and remind yourself of all the great things you have achieved so far. Ensure your self-talk is positive and cheer yourself on like you would a close friend.

3. Purpose

Purpose is the reason why something is done, created or exists. Jack Canfield, the author of **Chicken Soup for the Soul,** says: "Clarify your purpose. What is the why behind everything you do? When we know this in life or design, it is very empowering, and the path is very clear."

Being clear on your purpose pushes away fear and self-doubt. It keeps you accountable, removes distractions and narrows your focus. It's like a compass that encourages you to keep moving. When you combine belief with purpose, you can be bold.

If you're trying to elevate your communication through vulnerability, you may have an initial purpose, such as trying to get a better clickthrough rate on your website. If you're a CEO, it might be to motivate your team for the year ahead. But there needs to be a deeper level of purpose, what some might call a high purpose, in your work to share your hero's journey. Maybe your mission is to help others achieve their potential or to build a great company that employs thousands of people. If you can tap into your higher purpose, you tap into your truth. And when you tap into your truth, you share yourself with intent—not to manipulate—but to connect at a deep and authentic level. Your conviction will shine, and people will see you share with an open heart.

Your purpose is unique to you and makes you feel alive. It's creative, energised and limitless. It allows you to thrive and be powerful. There is no right or wrong purpose. The only person who can stop you being on purpose is you. So, by sharing these parts of you, your "scars" become beauty spots and you radiate authentic energy. You truly hit a sweet spot with your communication.

Safety and the need to belong

Not only is it vital for you as a leader to feel safe being vulnerable; you also need to ensure your team feels safe to be vulnerable, too. Safety is everything when it comes to building trust in your team. Without it, they lose a sense of belonging. Our need to belong to a tribe is primal and key to our survival. In fact, research suggests that a sense of belonging motivates human behaviour more than our physiological and safety needs.[3]

This need has implications for the way people are physically connected—or disconnected—at work. Hiring managers expect a 168% increase in the amount of work done by flexible talent (temporary, freelance or agency workers) in 10 years.[4] This puts even greater pressure on leaders to build a strong sense of community, connection and trust in their tribe.

Vulnerability and social media

In the age of social media, it's not hard to find out about the character of the people we deal with in business. We can simply look them up on LinkedIn and Facebook. That's why it's so important we take control of our online presence and key to this is being comfortable with being vulnerable.

Up until now, leaders have been able to hide behind and rely on the brand of their businesses and organisations to build trust for them, attract great talent and form tribes. This is especially true of countries where the tall poppy syndrome exists, such as the UK and Australia. Positioning and promoting yourself are seen as shameful things to do. This way of thinking needs to change.

For example, about five years ago, I had a client whose executive coach practically dragged him to me so I could help him market himself. He said he couldn't think of anything worse than self-promotion. He was the CEO of a global multinational and was trying to fast-track the growth of the business. His coach could see the best way to do this was to leverage the power of LinkedIn, so I wrote his LinkedIn profile. Initially, he felt incredibly uncomfortable about his face and profile being used online for business growth. Fortunately, he came to see the power of this strategy and today, he is an avid user of Instagram for a new business, has a YouTube channel and even his own podcast!

It is now a little more commonplace for organisations to leverage a CEO's profile for business growth, but it's still not the cultural norm in Australia and the UK. The sooner we embrace the United States' lead on this, the better. And if leaders and organisations can do it before it becomes mainstream, it will make more of an impact.

QUESTIONS

1. How easy or hard is it for you to share your challenges, experiences and stories of failure with others?

2. How do you react when someone you admire shares their experiences of hardship?

3. What holds you back from sharing your own experiences?

4. What makes it easy?

5. What makes it hard?

6. What can you do to foster an environment of safety in your team or tribe to help others be vulnerable without shame?

7. If you have successfully managed to create a safe space for people to be themselves and become high performing, how do you plan to maintain that safety?

NOTES

[1] https://janeandersonspeaks.com/women-with-influence/

[2] Brene Brown, "The Power of Vulnerability," TED, June 2010. https://www.ted.com/talks/brene_brown_on_vulnerability?language=en

[3] Kendra Cherry, "How the Need to Belong Influences Human Behaviour and Motivation," Verywell Mind, January 10, 2019. https://www.verywellmind.com/what-is-the-need-to-belong-2795393

[4] Lydia Dishman, "Remote work is 'the new normal,'" Fast Company, February 28, 2018. https://www.fastcompany.com/40537399/remote-work-is-the-new-normal

Humility |

CHAPTER TEN

"The difference between a good
leader and a great leader is
humility."

– *Jim Collins*

Jeff Bezos is the founder and CEO of Amazon and the wealthiest man on the planet.

When Bezos first started Amazon, he created his desk from a door purchased from Home Depot. At the time, doors were cheaper than desks, so he decided to buy a door and put legs on it. Right up until 1999, when Amazon stock was valued at $10 billion, the company still used doors as desks.

Today, Amazon employees in corporate roles and fulfilment centres use an upgraded version of the door desks. Frugality remains one of Amazon's leadership principles. "Constraints breed resourcefulness, self-sufficiency and invention," reads an Amazon leadership principle on its website. [1]

Bezos even uses the symbol of the humble desk door to recognise employees who think of cost-saving ideas, presenting them with a personally signed miniature desk called the "Door Desk Award". Recently, the award was given to three employees who suggested the company use gift bags instead of gift wrap for presents, saving Amazon millions of dollars.[2] Amazon also explains how anyone can build a door desk in six steps.[3]

When you are modest, you create a team environment free of ego. You share your knowledge with people in a helpful way to educate and change their world. People feel at ease in your presence; they know you're not going to make them feel stupid. It was Coco Chanel who said, "Modesty is the highest elegance."

If you aren't modest, people feel manipulated. How can they trust you if it appears you're giving them the run-around or pushing an agenda?

A study conducted by Don E. Davis found that modesty is a subdomain of humility.[4] Modesty is about being down to earth, practical and straight with people. Nobody likes a show-off who spouts jargon and makes others feel inadequate. But is modesty alone enough to breed a humble leader?

HUMBLE LEADERSHIP

FOCUS ON OTHERS

Domineering	Humble

CLOSED-MINDED ——————————————|—————————————— OPEN-MINDED

Arrogant	Narcissistic

FOCUS ON SELF

© Jane Anderson

How does humble leadership compare to other leadership traits and styles? In my experience, there are two variables at play: where a leader focuses their attention (focus on others/focus on self) and how curious they are (close-minded/open-minded).

• Narcissistic

A leader with a narcissistic approach to motivating others may be open-minded and curious about new ways of doing things, but their lens remains focussed on what will benefit them. They are often able to connect with people more than an arrogant or domineering leader can, but members of a tribe or team are usually not 100% sure if they can truly trust them. Leadership expert Michael Maccoby talks about the productive narcissist, citing Steve Jobs as an example.[5] In some organisations, this type of leader works because they can get things done. The challenge is to keep their narcissistic trait in check. Having a group of mentors and trusted colleagues to advise them can work well.

• Arrogant

On the surface, an arrogant leader can seem similar to a domineering leader, but they are different. The key difference is their attention, curiosity and consideration for others. Arrogant leaders are focussed on what they can gain and how they will benefit. They lack openness to others' ideas. Often, an arrogant leader is a less developed leader in the early stages of their leadership journey. They may not be aware of how they impact or are perceived by others, and may benefit from some formal leadership training. When working with arrogant leaders, I try to test their level of openness, curiosity and attention to others. I may ask questions such as, "When was the last time you ran your engagement survey? What are your current engagement scores? How often do you gain feedback on your performance?" If they answer these questions readily and have systems in place, it indicates something else drives their arrogance. If they don't answer them readily, I follow up with, "Is that something you would consider doing in future?"

• Domineering

This type of leader is what you might call a "bossy boots". While their attention is outward focussed, it's still linked to their internal drivers and ideas, with little input sought from others. Rather than trying to create a culture of collaboration, innovation and inclusion, they focus on validating their own beliefs and leadership approach. Depending on their level of maturity and training, they may be able to change their approach if they can accept the need to change is not a sign of their incompetence. It can be difficult for this type of leader to have a personal board of directors advising them, as they struggle to be open to learning. Quite often, they fail to build trust because they have difficulty trusting others. They are driven by fear—fear of losing money, status or control. A question I ask them is, "Who do you go to for advice? Whom do you listen to? Who are your mentors?" These questions usually give some insight into whether they can loosen their control and surrender to the leadership of another.

• Humble

This type of leader is focussed on "attention out". Ego takes a back seat. They are curious and not afraid to be wrong or admit they don't know something. They are more focussed on the transformation of others, helping them grow through their challenges. This approach fosters innovation, creativity and inclusion. It's a disarming type of leadership that is particularly powerful during times of change. Jim Collins, author of **Good to Great,** calls this Level 5 Leadership.[6] While a Level 5 Leader is ambitious, they're far more focussed on the cause, the organisation and the purpose than themselves.

The critical point to remember is that energy, attention, ego and power are the fundamental elements of leadership. It's essential when building trust to be mindful of these elements and continue to find ways to raise your level of self-awareness. You also need to manage these traits in emerging talent.

Humility alone does not solve all trust issues. Combining it with resolve and tenacity—qualities that underpin credibility—allows leaders to steer their teams and organisations through unchartered territory and transformational change.

Power is so yesterday

With the rise of the #metoo movement, the issue of power wielded by those in influential roles is under scrutiny. Thirty years ago, before the rise of the internet and social media, brand and reputation management was relatively contained. Hollywood's issues regarding the abuse of power were not discussed in the public domain. Today, you could be in the middle of nowhere and not personally know anyone in Hollywood, yet you'll undoubtedly hear about these issues.

For the first time, KPMG's Global CEO Outlook report for 2017 identified brand as one of the top three issues in the future for CEOs.[7] In the past, it's been noted as an issue but has never ranked inside the top 10. The question being asked is, "Who are our leaders really?" Organisations that have leaders with integrity have nothing to worry about. But what does it mean for the future of organisations that don't?

Simply teaching leaders how to behave professionally isn't enough. The question for CEOs, HR managers and those engaging in leadership development is: "How do we balance the concepts of power and authority in leadership roles with teaching leaders to be respectful, curious and humble?"

The future of work and leadership requires a new approach. We need to shift from the pervasive command-and-control style of leadership to one of curiosity, collaboration and creativity. In fact, with the rise of smart machines and the prediction that up to 40% of jobs in the next 15-20 years will be replaced by artificial intelligence, humility has been identified as the number-one skill for the future of work.[8]

So, how do we achieve this new leadership style?

We need to remove our ego. Or, as leading positive psychology scientist Dr Barbara Fredrickson calls it, our "cocoon of self-absorption".

138 • TRUSTED / JANE ANDERSON

Humble leadership is the new power

Humble leaders are the leaders of tomorrow. They don't assume they know everything. They don't assume ultimate control over everyone else. They are empowered and powerful, but this power is achieved differently than in the past.

Humble leaders connect with others at a human level. They're open-minded and collaborative. They listen to others. They create an atmosphere of trust, respect and equality. Everyone and every business can succeed under humble leadership.

Humility connects people. It attracts customers so you don't have to hustle for them. It connects teams so they collaborate, use initiative and improve performance.

Humility is often perceived as a personality trait, so it is overlooked or brushed aside by many leadership programs. The challenge for many leaders is that when they get to the point of feeling confident in their role, they rarely explore it further, thinking confidence and engagement are the winning factors. If you've reached that level of confidence, no doubt you've built trust with your people. But there's more to come—you're only half-way to developing your full leadership potential.

Humble leaders are highly trusted and ideal for driving change, innovation and performance. They display the following six traits:

1. Real leadership

How do you demonstrate your values? Are your values congruent with your actions? If they are, people will perceive you as being authentic. They're more likely to trust you and want to work with you. Essentially, authenticity, or being real, is your personal brand. Do you walk your talk? Do you deliver what you say you do?

If you aren't authentic, you aren't convincing. You undermine your leadership and lose the confidence of your people. As leadership expert John Maxwell says, "Leaders become great not because of their power, but because of their ability to empower others."

2. Understanding and empathy

Harper Lee's novel **To Kill a Mockingbird,** published in 1960, chronicles lawyer Atticus Finch's defence of a wrongfully convicted black man in Depression-era Alabama. Adored for his courage and integrity, Atticus has become one of the most iconic literary heroes of the 20th century. In the book, he says: "You never really understand a person until you consider things from his point of view ... until you climb in his skin and walk around in it."

When you focus on others rather than yourself, you begin to understand and share their feelings. You earn their respect. People want to work with you because they have faith that you act with compassion and conviction. They value your consideration for the challenges they face.

Empathy is not the same as understanding. Empathy is the ability to share and experience the feelings, thoughts and experiences of another. Understanding is more about insight into what is going on within that experience for the person, what is causing it and what needs to be done to improve the situation.

According to the Centre for Creative Leadership, cultivating leaders' compassion, empathy and listening skills is key to motivating teams.[9] When you have empathy, you're sensitive to others' needs. You're also more likely to be proactive. This means instead of dealing with problems after they arise, you prevent or anticipate them; thus, saving time, money and headaches.

If you don't have empathy, you're likely to base your decisions on assumptions. This is an unhelpful way to lead. People will feel you don't care about their issues, which creates friction and mistrust.

3. Vulnerability

Don't be afraid to show your true self. As discussed in Chapter 9, people relate to vulnerability; it shows you're human.

If you try to show others that you're perfect all the time, you shame them. They think, "I'm not as good as you." They'll feel they will never be able to measure up and you will struggle to make a connection with them. There will always be something missing, and you might not be able to put your finger on it.

As Brene Brown says, "Vulnerability is the birthplace of innovation, creativity and change." It's important to admit when you're wrong. Tell stories of your own challenges, weaknesses and fears. Show people you're imperfect. This creates permission for them to be imperfect, too. As a result, you build strong connections that are difficult to replicate and hard to break.

4. Sincerity

As Joan of Arc left Vaucouleurs to begin her mission to save France on February 23, 1429, a woman asked her, "How can you make such a journey when on all sides are soldiers?" To which Joan replied: "Je n'ai pas peur, c'est pour cela que je fus nais," or, "I am not afraid, I was born for this!"

Sincere people are the trailblazers. They focus on what is right in the world. They have a mindset of abundance, focus on a higher purpose and don't fear failure as much as others.

Sincere leaders are curious, truthful and transparent. When you are sincere, people see you as genuine. They're more likely to want to build a rapport with you. You demonstrate that while you are forging your path in accordance with your values, you are still considerate of the needs of others.

If you don't show sincerity, people will see you as manipulative, acting purely out of self-interest. They will second-guess everything you do and disconnect through lack of trust.

5. Honesty

Dr Pete Stebbins, organisational psychologist and high-performance expert, talks about the importance of psychological safety in his book, **Level Up!** Psychological safety is the belief that a person can share their ideas, concerns and questions without fear of negative consequences, such as ridicule or contempt.

A place of psychological safety is one of openness. Your relationships and work culture must be steeped in honesty and respect. Your people need to feel safe being open and direct with you and know they won't lose face by speaking up. When honesty is seen as a tool for improvement, it can have a significant positive impact on your team's performance.

As Warren Buffet said, "Honesty is a very expensive gift. Don't expect it from cheap people." If you don't foster honesty amongst your team, and if you aren't honest yourself, you demonstrate that you don't care. People may think you're out to manipulate them, generating anxiety and fear.

6. Equality

Equality means a culture of fairness. It's how humble leaders create a truly powerful connection between themselves and their team.

Equality comes from elevating others and removing barriers. It is achieved through simple things, such as being courteous and shining the light on others. It's also achieved by ensuring everyone feels they are on the same level and no one is better than anyone else. As American lawyer, politician and orator Robert Ingersoll said, "We rise by lifting others."

A humble leader does not see themselves on a pedestal, and they aren't afraid to get their hands dirty. They don't consider themselves above getting on the "shop floor" and helping when required. When there is a culture of equality, people feel valued. There's no rivalry or competing agendas. There is a sense of fairness and your judgement is trusted.

If you don't create a culture of equality, morale nosedives and favouritism rears its ugly head, which impacts your effectiveness as a leader. Cliques form, performance suffers, and you will lose respect.

So, if you have been through your foundational leadership development and are feeling confident in your role, it might be time to consider levelling up into your humility. The most important thing is to start your humble leadership journey now, so you are well-placed for future success; for you, your teams, your organisation and society as a whole.

QUESTIONS

1. Think of the leaders you admire the most. What do you think has made them powerful?

2. How many of those leaders possess the trait of humility?

3. Of those who do, what specific behaviours do they engage in to show their humility?

4. What challenges your ego the most?

5. When does it get in the way?

6. What strategies do you use to manage your ego?

7. How do you promote humility in your team, tribe or community?

NOTES

[1] https://www.amazon.jobs/en/principles

[2] Ali Montag, "Jeff Bezos' first desk at Amazon was a door with four-by-fours for legs – here's why it still is today," Make It, January 23, 2018. https://www.cnbc.com/2018/01/23/jeff-bezos-first-desk-at-amazon-was-made-of-a-wooden-door.html

[3] "How to build your own Amazon door desk," Amazon, January 16, 2018. https://blog.aboutamazon.com/working-at-amazon/how-to-build-your-own-amazon-door-desk?linkId=47161376

[4] Daryl R. Van Tongeren, Joshua Stafford, Joshua N. Hook, Jeffrey D. Green, Don E. Davis and Kathryn A. Johnson, "Humility attenuates negative attitudes and behaviors toward religious out-group members," The Journal of Positive Psychology, September 15, 2014. https://www.tandfonline.com/doi/abs/10.1080/17439760.2015.1037861

[5] Michael Maccoby, "A forceful passion," The Washington Post, January 29, 2010. http://views.washingtonpost.com/leadership/panelists/2010/01/a-forceful-passion.html

[6] "Level 5 Leadership," Jim Collins. https://www.jimcollins.com/concepts/level-five-leadership.html

[7] "Disrupt and grow – 2017 Global CEO Outlook," KPMG International, 2017. https://assets.kpmg/content/dam/kpmg/xx/pdf/2017/06/2017-global-ceo-outlook.pdf

[8] Ed Hess, "Humility: The No. 1 Job Skill Needed For The Smart Machine Age," Forbes, May 18, 2015. https://www.forbes.com/sites/darden/2015/05/18/humility-the-1-job-skill-needed-for-the-smart-machine-age/#6a58a33d6c06

[9] William A. Gentry, Todd J. Weber and Golnaz Sadri, "Empathy in the Workplace: A Tool for Effective Leadership," Center for Creative Leadership, April 2007. https://www.ccl.org/wp-content/uploads/2015/04/EmpathyInTheWorkplace.pdf

CHAPTER ELEVEN

Inclusivity |

"Coming together is a beginning.
Keeping together is progress.
Working together is success."

– Henry Ford

As I mentioned in Chapter 6, I grew up in Lismore in northern New South Wales. It's 30 km from the beach and is a commercial hub for the Northern Rivers region. At the time, Lismore had a much smaller population and the only private high school between Tweed Heads and Grafton.

My family was white and middle class. My dad was an accountant and mum looked after us until my youngest sister started school. My best friend's parents were pig farmers and her mother ran the methadone clinic in Nimbin, dealing with drug addicts.

What I loved about growing up in Lismore was the cultural diversity. I went to school with beach bums, indigenous people, hippies, skaters, farmers and sports nuts. We were all so different, yet integrated so well. The result was that judgement was removed. No one cared what you owned, where you lived or what car you drove. All that mattered was whether you were a "good bloke". It was a highly connected place—you couldn't hide and people knew if you did the wrong thing.

I noticed other towns closer to the coast were more focussed on status, money, houses and cars. They were judgemental, but Lismore wasn't.

Since then, the population in these areas has exploded and so has the number of schools. As a result, there has been social segregation of sorts. The same thing happens when organisations grow. They become more segmented as the challenge to recruit and find great talent changes.

Cultural diversity in the workplace is achieved when companies are open to employing people from different backgrounds, regardless of race, religion or culture. In fact, studies show that culturally diverse companies can increase their bottom line by 19%.[1]

When leaders and companies are inclusive, they experience a range of benefits, including:

• **Reputation.** Employer brand reputation in the market is competitive. Anything that can attract and retain talent gives an organisation an advantage when competing for talent. Inclusivity builds a greater trust in the brand and is more likely to encourage potential talent to consider making a move to that business, especially in a tight job market.

• **Productivity.** Tunnel vision is reduced when an organisation has a diverse range of people with different opinions, experiences, challenges and biases. It opens mindsets to new questions and ideas, bringing fresh, new ways of working to boost productivity. A survey undertaken by Ottaviano and Peri found a more multicultural urban environment drives positive economic value.[2]

• **Reduces uncertainty.** In the future of work, organisations and leaders must deal with rapid change. The utilisation of human capital and finding the best and fastest ways to leverage skills are critical. The old ways of doing business don't work anymore. Sometimes, even the methods that worked last quarter won't work this quarter. It's an uncertain time, and leaders often fear feedback from their team, not wanting to appear or feel incompetent. But by increasing inclusion and aligning with a culture of equality and purpose, leaders' uncertainty is replaced with a sense of belonging. Trust and engagement drive growth.

• **Profitability.** A 2013 survey undertaken by the Center for Talent Innovation found that 48 per cent of companies in the US with more diversity at a senior management level improved their market share on the previous year. Only 33 per cent of companies with less diverse management reported similar growth.[3] So, there's no doubt diversity increases business growth, which, ultimately, is the goal of any leader.

• **Engagement.** A culture of inclusion and diversity creates greater respect, trust and engagement in teams and organisations.[4] People are more willing to listen to each other, they feel more cared for, they help each other more and are encouraged to be themselves. Team member confidence skyrockets, which is especially important if you're trying to increase the number of women in leadership roles. In the words of Michael Novak, author of more than 40 books on the philosophy and theology of culture: "Unity in diversity is the highest possible attainment of a civilisation, a testimony to the most noble possibilities of the human race. This attainment is made possible through passionate concern for choice, in an atmosphere of social trust."

Nembhard and Edmondson first defined inclusive leadership as a relationship style that always accepts the differences of various members.[5] Meanwhile, Carmeli et al. (2010) emphasised that "inclusive leadership refers to leaders who exhibit openness, accessibility, and availability in their interactions with followers."[6] While diversity is about compliance and targets, inclusion is more about growth, connection and individuality.

According to a study of 329 team members from 105 teams across six cities in China, inclusive leadership was positively correlated with employee voice behaviour at the individual level and team performance at the team level.[7] Essentially, the study found that a mix of transactional and transformational leadership was key to making teams work effectively.

So, how can leaders foster greater inclusivity to build trust in organisations at work each day:

• **Transactional.** Ensuring teams have the technical skills to complete the tasks at hand.

• **Transformational.** Supporting team members, listening and helping them become their best version of themselves. Listen, show you are, help your team members out, encourage people to be their authentic self.

So, it's not enough to simply have diversity in the workforce or your team; as a leader, you need to know how to make your team leverage to create high performance and gain a competitive advantage. Research suggests that "organisations that practise inclusion, as well as diversity, are able to experience high levels of collaboration, engagement and retention, which provide a competitive advantage."[8]

To foster greater inclusion in your teams, tribe and organisation, you need to focus on:

1. Mission and values. If your tribe is not aligned with the overall purpose and values of your organisation, they'll never truly feel part of the business. Your mission should showcase what you stand for, and your tribe should feel inspired to achieve it.

2. Employer branding. Ensure your employer branding reflects the value of inclusivity. Work on your branding by sharing stories from a diverse range of employees, ensure you have flexible working arrangements for parents and target more women for leadership roles.

High ↑		Adapted from *The Guide for Inclusive Leaders*, 2006

Competitive Advantage: Low Collaboration: Low Morale: Low Engagement: Low Retention: Low	Competitive Advantage: High Collaboration: High Morale: High Engagement: High Retention: High
A	**D**
B	**C**
Competitive Advantage: Average Collaboration: Average Morale: Average Engagement: Average Retention: Average	Competitive Advantage: Low Collaboration: Low Morale: High Engagement: High Retention: High

Diversity (vertical axis: Low → High)

Inclusion (horizontal axis: Low → High)

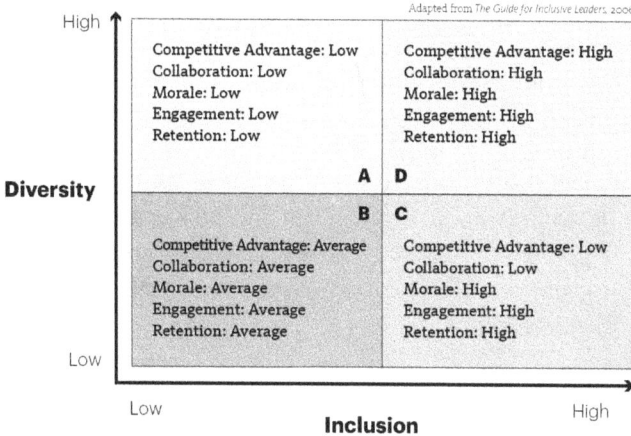

Source: *Janakiraman, 2011, p.3*

3. Communication. Share details of operational performance and plans for the future with your team. Let them feel included in the direction and decisions of the business. Initiate "town hall" meetings, where employees can meet and ask questions of senior managers. Furthermore, find ways to collaborate with teams cross-functionally. This will reduce silos and create more collective ideas, reducing groupthink.

4. Leadership. Your leadership team should role-model inclusive behaviour. Consider creating inclusion and diversity training as part of your leadership development programs. This training should encompass empathic leadership. The challenge is that your leaders will already think they're inclusive—no one wants to be sexist, racist or homophobic. But their role in shaping the culture of your organisation must be emphasised, and you need to educate them about unconscious bias, empathy and understanding. Your employees need to feel they have a future in your organisation; if they look at their leaders and feel they could never reach the same heights, you will lose them. Your leaders need to be able to recognise this early and ensure people feel they belong.

5. Onboarding. Review induction programs to ensure they explain policies on diversity. These programs must be rolled out not only to new staff but also to existing teams. Policies must specifically explain how employees can be more inclusive in the workplace, and even ask them what practices were effective in other organisations they've worked in.

6. Engagement scores. If you're in an organisation, you may like to consider measuring or surveying your teams. This can be done while undertaking engagement scores. If you work with clients on a regular basis, you may decide to use other platforms, such as the Net Promoter Score, which measures customer satisfaction.

7. Be mindful of quotas. Just because you may have reached diversity targets doesn't mean you have created a sense of belonging. Inclusion, while it goes hand in hand with diversity, is quite different. It's an ongoing process that requires continual leadership feedback and asking questions such as, "Who else should we invite to this meeting?", "Have I created an environment where each person can thrive, feel safe and contribute in a meaningful way?" It means taking the time to understand team dynamics, how people operate at their best and how they work with conflict.

8. Create shared experiences. In his book, *Power Vs Force,* David Hawkins says the antidote to fear is joy. People fear being removed and rejected by their tribe, so, as leaders, our job is to find creative ways to increase joy and connection in our tribes. My partner Mark's team members often participate in events and go on holidays as part of their social club. They've even been to New Zealand and on hiking trips to Nepal!

Here are some other factors to consider when creating an inclusive environment:

• **Include non-alcoholic drinks at events.** Not everyone drinks alcohol.

• **Seek feedback and input from people.** Listening to your tribe sends a powerful message that they're valued.

• **Consider what your executive team looks like.** Does it reflect the diversity you want to build in your organisation?

• **Provide nursing rooms for mothers.** This sends a message of empathy and understanding to female employees who are also managing life with a baby.

• **Ensure job descriptions have gender-neutral language.** Update "him" or "her" to "they", for example.

• **Be mindful of job descriptions.** Instead of merely listing qualities and skills, ensure job descriptions cover the results and outcomes you want people to achieve in their roles.

• **Include merit-based processes in your recruitment.** Ensure those recruiting talent are fair and equitable when recruiting. Teach them how to give constructive feedback to unsuccessful candidates.

• **Make sure everyone shares clean-up duties.** Have a roster for the weekly kitchen clean-up and make sure everyone has a turn.

• **Allow flexible work hours.** Find ways to make it easier for people to work. Sometimes people have commitments—such as elderly family members or health issues—that can make working 9-5 a challenge, yet they are fully committed to their job.

• **Check the types of magazines you have in your waiting area.** Ensure they're relevant to your industry.

• **Review the careers page on your website.** Do your employee stories and branding align? Is there diversity in their backgrounds and circumstances? Even a sentence stating your commitment to creating a diverse and inclusive organisation speaks volumes.

• **Give each person the opportunity to speak without interruption at meetings.** Research shows that women are interrupted more than men, but everyone in the workplace deserves to be heard.

These activities may seem inconsequential, but they all add up. By undertaking even just a few of these inclusive activities, you will foster greater feelings of trust as a leader. Your tribe will also be more forgiving when things don't go to plan.

QUESTIONS

1. What blend of ethnicity, religion and gender exists in your team or organisation?

2. If you asked your team members, would they agree with you?

3. What procedures and policies do you have in place to reduce unconscious bias in the recruitment process and promotion of talent?

4. Who in your organisation is a champion of diversity and inclusion?

5. What are your business goals for the next 3-5 years?

6. Have you created diversity and inclusion targets to attract and retain talent?

7. What specific actions do you need to take from here?

NOTES

[1] Anna Powers, "A Study Finds That Diverse Companies Produce 19% More Revenue," Forbes, June 27, 2018. https://www.forbes.com/sites/annapowers/2018/06/27/a-study-finds-that-diverse-companies-produce-19-more-revenue/#4c3e3b4b506f

[2] Gianmarco I.P. Ottaviano and Giovanni Peri, "The economic value of cultural diversity: evidence from US cities," Journal of Economic Geography, Oxford University Press, vol. 6(1), pages 9-44, January 2006. https://www.nber.org/papers/w10904

[3] Oliver Ralph and Laura Noonan, "Diversity brings boost to profitability," Financial Times, April 4, 2017. https://www.ft.com/content/1bc22040-1302-11e7-80f4-13e067d5072c

[4] "The role of diversity practices and inclusion in promoting trust and employee engagement," Deloitte, May 2015. https://www2.deloitte.com/au/en/pages/human-capital/articles/role-diversity-practices-inclusion-trust-employee-engagement.html

[5] Ingrid M. Nembhard and Amy C. Edmondson, "Making it safe: the effects of leader inclusiveness and professional status on psychological safety and improvement efforts in health care teams," Journal of Organizational Behaviour, 27, 941-966, November 2006

[6] Abraham Carmeli, Roni Reiter-Palmon and Enbal Ziv, "Inclusive leadership and employee involvement in creative tasks in the workplace: the mediating role of psychological safety," Creativity Research Journal, 22, 250-260, August 10, 2010

[7] Lei Qi and Bing Liu, "Effects of Inclusive Leadership on Employee Voice Behavior and Team Performance: The Mediating Role of Caring Ethical Climate," Frontiers in Communication, September 27, 2017. https://pdfs.semanticscholar.org/6575/56ad40532af2dbod0e4946cb4ba0c33a0f2e.pdf

[8] Malini Janakiraman, "Inclusive Leadership – Critical for Competitive Advantage," Mercer. https://mobilityexchange.mercer.com/Insights/article/Inclusive-Leadership-Critical-for-Competitive-Advantage

CHAPTER TWELVE

Transparency |

"A lack of transparency results
in distrust and a deep sense of
insecurity."

– Dalai Lama

How to humanise a brand for trust, transparency and business growth

I live on the south side of Brisbane in an area on the M1 motorway. There are several yellow silhouettes along some roadworks near Eight Mile Plains, which have been part of the Gateway Motorway upgrade for the past year or so. It turns out the silhouettes are part of a safety movement created by civil construction company Fulton Hogan. Other construction businesses have adopted the initiative as well.

The reason they're there is to protect some ground-monitoring equipment. The company tried to flag the equipment, but it kept getting knocked over. One of the team members said, "Well, they wouldn't get knocked over if a human being was standing there."

So, the company decided to create figurines to act as markers. They tapped into the psychology of safety and shame, getting people to draw parallels between the equipment and workers on site. They assigned the name of a real worker to each yellow silhouette, and if one was knocked over, the person who did it had to apologise to the real person, which created the link with safety. As a result, the amount of damage to onsite safety equipment was significantly reduced. The construction company has used the silhouettes for other projects as well.

What does this mean for leaders and organisations trying to tap into business growth?

Well, if you're leading a team within an organisation, you might not think you're an influencer. However, based on your role and responsibility, you have more influence on the business and team growth than you might think.

You see, you don't have to be in construction to use these principles as part of your strategy. With the shift towards growing businesses through social networks, using internal influencers such as leaders within the business is your secret weapon to supporting business growth. The benefits are enormous: not only can the organisation save money on marketing and PR, but you can also engage your team in the growth of the brand so they have more connection with the business and brand identity. You will not only attract more customers, but attract great talent who are often looking at your social profiles.

The impact if you don't use internal influencers? You continue to spend money on costly, time-consuming marketing activities, such as Google AdWords and search engine optimisation. Meanwhile, influencers are often sitting right under your nose at minimal cost.

For example, in 2014 I ran a superannuation campaign for a financial services organisation when there was a change in legislation. My team and I wrote the LinkedIn profiles of about 70 staff and taught them how to reach out to their connections. The organisation was on board with finding ways to educate their market. As a result, the company received 500 new leads from that campaign.

It's no secret that LinkedIn has incredible power. More than 60% of users have just under 1000 connections. And according to **Fast Company** magazine, the open rate of content from a personal account is eight times higher than the open rate of content from a business account.[1] This means each person in your team or organisation has the opportunity to become an influencer for your brand. The good news is that you don't have to coerce all your staff to be influencers; even tapping into one of them can be a valuable business-growth activity.

There are typically four levels of opportunity within an organisation to humanise a brand and access new markets. Each has a different purpose and value proposition to be effectively leveraged:

	PURPOSE	POSITIONING
CEO	Captivate	• Talent • Clients • Opportunities	• Uniqueness • Contribution
Executive	Credibility	• Opportunity • Collaboration • Cultural fit
Managers	Culture	• Talents • Clients
Business Development	Customer	

© Jane Anderson

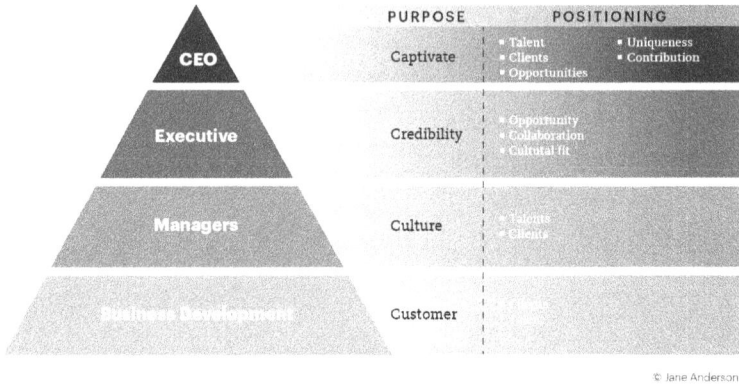

Level 1: Business Development: Customer Connection

These are people who have access to vast social connections and followings that can be used for business-to-business growth. For example, if you have a sales team, use your sales team's LinkedIn profiles to grow the employer brand and access new clients.

Level 2: Managers: Culture

The role of managers and leaders is to attract talent. This means tapping into LinkedIn social networks to access ideal talent for the organisation. This is particularly important when you consider that 97% of job seekers validate their potential employer online as part of their job search.

Level 3: Executive: Credibility

These are roles that set the tone and culture of an organisation. They also attract talent and opportunities to the organisation. Typically, these team members have great connections and need to have a professional digital presence. They may also be on tender documents and need to be easily validated by those engaging with and assessing them.

Level 4: CEO: Captivation

A founder will generally have a stronger connection to the organisation's brand and identity, as opposed to the CEO, who was appointed to the organisation. But both can still be ambassadors. The CEO is the rainmaker. It's about sharing content, having a profile that attracts talent and opportunities, and setting the tone. The CEO is the most leveraged profile of all the influencers in an organisation. They need to captivate, engage and inspire customers and talent to take the next step and be part of their vision.

The key is not to coerce or make people become influencers through their LinkedIn, Twitter or other social media profiles. Employees own their LinkedIn and social media profiles, and it is up to them to be involved.

Becoming an influencer via social media is voluntary; you can only put guidelines in place to encourage people. And yes, there is some brand risk regarding how that person is perceived online. However, if done well, using the social media profiles of your team members can be a cost-effective way of creating a human connection with your brand, building visibility and trust, accessing new clients and gaining a competitive edge in your industry.

Psychological safety

Transparency in teams creates psychological safety, which we discussed in Chapter 10. Psychological safety is critical to building the trust and growth of leaders and organisations.

Dr Amy Silver, a Melbourne-based expert in psychological safety, says:

Psychological safety precedes innovation, honest communication, agile behaviours, engagement and enables individuals to tap into hidden potential. All good things. Feeling psychologically unsafe is, in comparison, not a good thing. It results in fear, overthinking, under speaking and groupthink. All bad things. If we want to create a culture that grows, there is no advantage to people feeling psychologically unsafe.

But interestingly, when it comes to tasks (rather than a global sense of safety), it's different.

It will often be helpful to growth if people are stretched and challenged in their tasks. By enabling a (supervised) level of task insecurity in a psychologically safe environment, we create the opportunity to learn and innovate. By challenging individuals with tasks, we create the space for a growth spurt in capability, empowerment and achievement, even if it is accompanied by discomfort.

When people are not stretching in tasks, there will be no growth, even in a psychologically safe environment. This is because people get comfortable, and comfortable has an impact on their efforts and their fulfilment.

So ...

Growth zone = psychologically safe environment + task stretch

No growth zone = psychologically safe environment + no task stretch.

No growth zone = psychological unsafe environment.[2]

So, the benefit of creating a psychologically safe space means you increase the stretch and growth zone of your tribe, thereby improving performance. Without psychological safety, their growth is reduced and so is performance.

Problem solving

Transparency and psychological safety are also vital to team members feeling comfortable enough to problem solve. Zeynep Ilgaz, president and founder of Confirm Biosciences and noted expert on leadership, highlights the importance of team involvement in problem-solving when she advises companies to "stop sugar-coating your communication. Include your employees in discussions about important business matters, and ask for their help in solving problems. They will rally around you, and this collaboration will strengthen your entire team."[3]

A great example of the effectiveness of collaborative problem-solving occurred in 2018 when Elon Musk tweeted that his company Tesla needed to deliver hundreds of cars to customers but didn't have the staff to deliver them. He called on existing customers (raving fans) to volunteer to deliver the vehicles, and they did.[4]

What better way to engage potential customers with your product and build their trust than by leveraging raving fans? People are more likely to trust you and your brand via real people who have had first-hand experiences of you.

How to increase transparency

There are many ways you can increase transparency as a leader to create greater trust and psychological safety in a team:

• **Create core values.** Identify and define the specific values and behaviours you want your tribe to uphold and engage in. Describe what these behaviours look like and be specific. Values and clearly defined behaviours give people a sense of safety: expectations are clear because they know the ground rules. As psychologist and author Dr Pete Stebbins says, *"Without ground rules, safety in a team is lost and performance suffers. Team members need to know how to call each other out on behaviour when it doesn't comply with core values."*

• **Be an open book.** Share the challenges you have faced in your career or business journey. We may be reluctant to be open about our experiences because we're afraid of appearing incompetent. But sharing your experiences is not about what happened; it's about what happened **next.** Equally, if you can't talk to your team about something confidential, let them know. Don't lie and say you don't know anything about it if you do. People will see through you, and it's not worth the reputation damage. It's also important to share your successes. When working with my coaching clients, I'm happy to share what the business turnover is so they know they're working with someone who has achieved what they want to achieve.

• **Be responsive.** If people have a problem, do something about it. Don't ignore it and hope it will go away. Answer their questions and nip the issue in the bud. A stitch in time saves nine, and people will feel confident that something will be done when they come to you with problems or challenges. They know their concerns won't fall on deaf ears.

• **Be open to others' opinions.** It pays to be curious to build transparency and trust. We don't always see our blind spots, so being open to others' perceptions and opinions is helpful. Even though you may have already decided on an outcome, it's never too late to listen to others' opinions, input or feedback. They will feel valued and heard.

• **Create a community.** When you have trust, you have power. What creates even more power is social proof that you are a leader of people, otherwise known as a community. All businesses have the opportunity to develop communities through influencers. This is because people buy from people they know, like and trust.

• **Ask questions.** By seeking feedback from your tribe, you'll gain greater insights and increase psychological safety. Asking questions creates a culture of openness. When others see you as the leader asking questions, they see you as humble and inclusive. You make it OK not to know everything.

• **Be honest and admit to mistakes.** It's important, as a leader, to tell the truth. If you or the organisation have done something incorrectly, you need to own up to it. Even better if you apologise if your mistake affected someone negatively. You'll gain much more credibility for your honesty and ethics. Trying to hide through cover-ups never works and will work against you in the long run.

• **Give credit to others.** People sometimes don't share their knowledge out of fear that someone else might take their idea. Be sure to shine a light on those

who do a great job. Be specific about what they did and acknowledge them
if they have been a critical contributor to the success of your team. It doesn't
take much to say thank you and highlight their contribution. They'll be more
likely to do it again!

QUESTIONS

1. How open are you with your team? Do you share the challenges you and the business experience? How do you know what to share and what not to share?

2. When your team comes to you with a significant problem or challenge, how quick are you to help them resolve it? Or do you ignore issues unless they rear their head again?

3. What specific actions do you take to include others' opinions?

4. How readily do you apologise and admit to your mistakes?

5. When was the last time you acknowledged someone for their work? How easy was it for you to do this?

6. How often do you ask your team for their input with challenges and issues?

7. In what other ways do you create a sense of belonging and psychological safety for your tribe?

NOTES

[1] Ryan Holmes, "How To Turn Your Entire Staff Into A Social Media Army," Fast Company, 2015. https://www.fastcompany.com/3053233/how-to-turn-your-entire-staff-into-a-social-media-army

[2] Amy Silver, "How To Use Psychological Safety In Cultures That Grow," September 26, 2017. http://www.dramysilver.com/silverlinings/

[3] William Arruda, "Five Ways To Identify A Company With A Culture Of Transparency," Forbes, March 11, 2018. https://www.forbes.com/sites/williamarruda/2018/03/11/five-ways-to-identify-a-company-with-a-culture-of-transparency/#1977ef1a4804

[4] Paul Roberts, "Tesla's true-believer owners volunteer to help Musk complete deliveries," The Seattle Times, October 5, 2018. https://www.seattletimes.com/business/teslas-true-believer-owners-volunteer-to-help-musk-make-delivery-deadline/?utm_content=buffer534e8&utm_medium=social&utm_source=twitter.com&utm_campaign=owned_buffer_biz

In Closing |

This book covers a lot of ground from what trust was in the past, to where it is today and its implications for the future of work. The concepts in the book are designed to start the conversation rather than be an exhaustive list, and to help you to consider how they may apply for you, your team and organisation as well as to consider what else builds trust for the people who matter in your world.

The ideas behind this book and the platform are designed to help give you a framework to consider, measure and gain insights into the areas you have strengths and other areas that are an opportunity to focus on and improve. As each area improves there is a continuous levelling up that occurs whether each day, quarter or year as part of making more conscious and intentional choices around trust in building your tribe.

The key to remember is not to be afraid to start small. Whilst the levelling up of trust may seem like a huge mountain to climb, it can just start with you. One conversation, one client, one team at a time. Take the lead and be the example that others can follow. From there the ripple of change begins.

I would love to hear how you go implementing the 9 key skills; please reach out to share your stories and examples to jane@jane-anderson.com.au.

WORK WITH JANE

"Within four weeks of making a couple of modest tweaks,
Jane Anderson's advice led to me increasing online
revenue by more than 10x! Simple, clear, direct strategies
that increase impact and influence."

– Dr Justin Coulson, Parenting Expert

With over 20 years' experience, and highly compassionate yet commercial in her approach, Jane has helped more than 50,000 leaders. She is a certified speaker and coach, and has been featured on Sky Business, The Today Show, The Age, The Sydney Morning Herald, BBC and Management Today.

The author of six books, Jane typically speaks at conferences, runs workshops, consults and coaches female leaders and influencers in how to communicate more powerfully and grow their businesses and careers. Her clients often come with the following challenges:

- How to build their personal brand and/or consulting business.
- How to lead their tribe or teams more effectively.
- Business growth, sales, marketing and communications strategy.

She also trains Business Coaches, Personal Branding Consultants and Marketing Assistants to become Certified Influencer Coach Practitioners.

Jane holds one of the top 1% viewed LinkedIn profiles and is the host of the "Jane Anderson Show" podcast.

She has been nominated for and won numerous industry awards for her expertise, including:
- International Stevie Awards for Coach & Entrepreneur of the Year 2018
- Nominated Telstra Business Awards 2014, 2016 & 2018
- Top 30 branding gurus globally
- Top 25 branding blogs
- Top 6 branding experts in Australia

CORPORATE CLIENTS HAVE INCLUDED:
Telstra, International Rice Research Institute, Wesfarmers, Amadeus, Virgin Australia, IKEA, LEGO, Mercedes-Benz, Australian Medical Association, Shell Energy and WorkCover.

GET INVOLVED

Speaking	Jane is a Certified Speaker and has spoken at more than 300 conferences and events globally. To find out how she can help you create a memorable experience at your next event, go to *https://janeandersonspeaks.com/personal-branding-keynote-speaker/*
Workshops	RJane delivers in-house workshops on LinkedIn, personal branding, trust, influence and leadership. To find out more about how she can help your teams and leaders achieve their potential, go to *https://janeandersonspeaks.com/programs/training/*
Women with Influence Women's Leadership Coaching	Are you a female leader or business owner and need help to grow your influence, presence and confidence? A great place to start is by attending one of the Women with Influence events in your local city. To find out when the next event is on nearest to you, go to *https://janeandersonspeaks.com/events/*
Public Workshops	Jane delivers a public workshop each year on Expert to Influencer and Trusted Methodology for Experts and Aspiring Practitioners. To find out about future dates, go to *https://janeandersonspeaks.com/programs/training/*
Online Programs	Join Jane's Personal Branding Institute and access training 24 hours per day, 7 days per week, on how to build your leadership brand and community. Jane also delivers her online program, Expert to Influencer, each quarter live. To find out upcoming dates, go to *http://jane-andersons-online-learning-academy.thinkific.com*
Facebook Community	Join Jane's Expert to Influencer Facebook community, where we talk all things communication for building influence, trust and leadership. *https://www.facebook.com/groups/experttoinfluencer/*

READ MORE OF JANE'S BOOKS

The old ways of growing a business have changed.

Social media has levelled the playing field and now it's easier than ever to compete with the big players in your industry.

Whether you're a Thought Leader, Trusted Advisor, Academic or Expert, the way you position and market yourself is now more important than ever.

This book will help you uncover the 12 secret activities to grow your business and opportunities.

Never has there been an opportunity for businesses and consultants to identify, engage and connect with their ideal audience like there is now with LinkedIn. By the end of this book, you will have the strategies you need to generate leads and grow your business using LinkedIn. You will be armed with practical steps that you can implement straight away to see real results. Your outcomes will be stronger, and you will lead the competition on this new playing field.

Discover how to create "corporation you" without being a tall poppy. We're no longer in the industrial or information age. We're now in the connection economy, where your ability to stand out, connect with others and position yourself in your career and business means security. It means you won't be left behind but instead be ahead of the pack. Companies and governments no longer want people who want jobs for life. They want innovation, ideas and networks to thrive in volatile economic times. We are bombarded with information and choices every day. Hard work alone doesn't cut it anymore.

We all hate selling ourselves, but interviews are one of those times when you can't be shy. You have to stand out from the crowd, and there's a way to give the panel what they want to hear without sounding like you're blowing your own trumpet. From this book, you will learn techniques to increase your confidence, how to anticipate the questions the panel might ask and how to practice in the lead-up to the big day.

www.ingramcontent.com/pod-product-compliance
Lightning Source LLC
Chambersburg PA
CBHW060311220326
41598CB00027B/4301